# THE EMPOWERMENT REVOLUTION

## FROM SELF-DOUBT TO SELF-MADE

### DR. STACEY KEVIN FRICK

Red Thread Publishing LLC. 2025

Red Falcon Press Imprint

Write to **info@redthreadbooks.com** if you are interested in publishing with Red Falcon Press. Learn more about publications or foreign rights acquisitions of our catalog of books: **www.redthreadbooks.com**

Paperback ISBN: 979-8-89294-031-3

Ebook ISBN: 979-8-89294-032-0

Cover Design: Red Thread Designs

Author Photo: @MIKEDUNNUSA for Celebrity Branding Agency

# CONTENTS

# FOREWORD
## BY LISA NICHOLS

When I first met Dr. Stacey Kevin Frick, I recognized something in him I've seen in very few people—a soul who isn't just doing the work but *living* it. I saw brilliant humility. I saw a man who doesn't just talk about transformation, he embodies it. And that's exactly what *The Empowerment Revolution* is. It's not just a book. It's a lived movement. An invitation. A new blueprint for becoming who you were *always meant to be.*

Now listen, before I stood on stages around the world, before I co-authored bestselling books, before anyone knew my name, I was a single mom on public assistance, barely able to look myself in the mirror. I didn't feel powerful. I didn't feel worthy. I felt like I had ruined every good thing I'd ever touched.

And then I rewrote those codes that had no place in the future I wanted for me and my child. That revolution didn't start on the outside. It started within. It started when I chose to *no longer be available for my own suffering.* It started when I decided to stop asking for permission to rise.

And it continued when I looked in the mirror, tears streaming down my face, and said, *"Lisa, I'm proud of you."*

That is the empowerment revolution. And that is what Dr. Frick invites you into; not surface change, but a full soul reclamation. A shedding of identities, expectations, and inherited beliefs that were never yours to carry. This book doesn't give you just more information, it gives you the activation you've been waiting for.

Dr. Frick's framework is both spiritual and practical, rooted in clinical experience and divine inspiration. He holds up a mirror and hands you the tools to stop shrinking, stop apologizing, and start becoming *dangerously free*.

This is the work that wakes you up and brings you home.

So if you're holding this book right now, I want to ask you a sacred question: Are you ready to be interrupted?

Because *The Empowerment Revolution* is going to interrupt your old story. It's going to interrupt your playing small. It's going to challenge you, stretch you, love you and ultimately liberate you.

I am deeply honored to stand beside Dr. Stacey Kevin Frick in this movement. His heart is big, his message is urgent, and this moment—right now—is your invitation.

Let the revolution begin!

With fierce love and faith in your becoming,

I'm your sister in the journey,

*Lisa Nichols*

**Motivational Speaker,**
**Bestselling Author,**
**Transformational Coach**

# INTRODUCTION

It was a frigid day in Germany as a little boy made his way home from school, crying tears that felt like icicles streaming down his face. The sting of his teacher's words still echoed fresh in his mind–words that seemed to seal his fate– that he would never amount to anything. He just wasn't smart enough.

One hundred years later, a young Black girl, whose family was stricken with poverty, did her best to thrive despite the repeated assaults she suffered at the hands of her cousin.

Twenty years after that, a three-year-old boy nearly died when his violent, alcoholic father lay on top of him, suffocating the breath from his body, delighting in each sign of struggle.

That discarded student was Albert Einstein.

That abused little girl was Oprah Winfrey.

And that toddler who was nearly killed by his father was me.

These stories all could have ended very differently. The characters could have allowed themselves to be defined by those incidents. They could have shrunken back, given up, and disappeared.

Instead, they embarked on a different journey. They rewrote their own stories into epic adventures and heroes' journeys. They made up their minds to quiet the critics, to release the trauma, and in doing so ignited an inner revolution–one that not only transformed their lives but changed the lives of others and the world at large.

They decided to rise, to reflect on the truths in their hearts, and to ultimately reshape their destinies.

The same outcome is possible for you, too.

Imagine waking up every day with a deep sense of confidence, purpose, and excitement about the future. Picture the freedom of knowing that you are in control of your life, capable of shaping your destiny, and free to make decisions that are in alignment with your true desires and values. This is what it feels like to live a life of empowerment, and taking charge of your fate feels nothing short of amazing.

Empowerment is the ultimate expression of personal freedom. It is the understanding that you are not a passive participant in life, subject to the whims of fate, but an active creator of your own experience. Living an empowered life means embracing your inherent power and potential, and creates a profound shift in how you perceive and experience the world around you. In this book, we will explore the incredible emotional, mental, and spiritual benefits that come with living a life of empowerment and the liberation that is possible.

In a world where most people arguably have more access to basic needs than ever before, many of us still operate from a place of survival rather than expansion. Despite our material advancements, persistent fear looms—the fear that we will not have enough, that we are not good enough, that failure is inevitable. The weight of this belief that life happens to us and that we are powerless to influence its direction can be paralyzing. This fear can trap us into inaction, even when we know exactly what we need to do to improve our circumstances.

Insecurity does not start with us; it has been programmed into us since before birth and reinforced by nearly every authority we encounter. These authorities—governments, religious institutions, families, societies, and the media—excel at telling us what success should look like and how we should behave to achieve it. Those who impose such standards and expectations often fail to consider each individual's unique nature and personal definition of success.

This disconnect between what we are *told* and what we actually *feel* creates an emotional landscape filled with fear, stress, frustration, anxiety, and an overwhelming sense of discomfort. Rather than expanding into our potential, we are tempted to shrink to fit a mold that was never designed for us.

The journey of this book is about breaking free from this fear-based mentality and unlocking all of the beautiful gifts inside you so you can realize a world of joy, fulfillment, and impact. This exploration is about embracing a mindset of expansion, rediscovering your personal power, and understanding that true success is deeply individual. We will dismantle your long-held limiting beliefs and reclaim the freedom to define success and happiness on your own terms. This is an invitation to shift from mere survival to thriving, from following someone else's script to authoring your own.

This point is where so many people stop. They recognize that something needs to change, but they stop at that awareness. Sometimes they stop because they don't know where to start. Sometimes they don't want to admit that they need some guidance. And sometimes, they believe that doing this type of work means that there is something inherently wrong with them.

"After all," they reason, "a healthy person wouldn't need to do personal development work."

Let me reframe that for you by suggesting you take a walk by your local gym. The gym is filled with people who are in top-notch shape—pillars of good health. No one says, "Wow, what a shame that they need to go to the gym." The gym is *how* they maintain that healthy body!

The same is true on your path from feeling stuck, stressed, and not good enough to step into your personal empowerment. Living a life of impact and fulfillment is anything but easy. It requires confronting deep-seated beliefs, embracing vulnerability, and committing to a process of continuous growth. Along the way, doubts will certainly surface. Challenges will test your resolve. You will face your fears, your ideals, and your values, and question everything you believe to be true. However, every step forward reclaims a piece of your true self, bringing you clarity, purpose, and joy. You will find courage in your vulnerability and strength in your surrender. The journey transforms not just how you view yourself, but how you interact with the world and how the world interacts with you, inevitably proving that the effort to live authentically is always worth it.

If you are standing at this crossroads between the past and the future, you have a choice to make. Will you continue struggling, doubting, and wishing for a different life? Or will you take the hero's journey to fight for the life you want and the future you deserve?

The first road is constructed by human failures, fears, and ego. That road leads to regret. The second road is constructed by universal laws and all the gifts that life has to offer and leads to your empowered destiny.

I hope you will walk with me on the second path, where the road is smoother and the scenery is breathtaking.

# CHAPTER 1
# DIGGING UP THE ROOT OF DISCOMFORT

---

*"The stories we tell literally make the world. If you want to change the world, you need to change your story."*

MICHAEL MARGOLIS

---

WHY DO SO MANY OF US FEEL UNCOMFORTABLE IN LIFE, AS THOUGH WE are constantly struggling to meet our needs? We strive to achieve goals, acquire material wealth, and attain meaning, but often find ourselves feeling incomplete, even when we succeed. What creates this persistent sense of limitation and despair?

If you have felt this nagging discomfort–the sense that you were plopped into the wrong life– and you're starting to worry that maybe you are destined to be unhappy, you must know two things.

The first is that none of it is your fault. You were programmed by your family, your religion, your government, and society to be a certain way, to fall in line, to accept the hand that was dealt to you. Up until now, your programming is all you've known.

However, while none of it is your fault, it is your responsibility to choose a different way forward; to release the shackles of this programming, programming which has nothing to do with who you are. Think of it this way- imagine you are a perfect and brand-new computer until people come along and install software that has viruses running through it. Suddenly, your brand-new, perfect system is corrupt. It wasn't your fault. You couldn't have known what kind of software was being programmed. The viruses have nothing to do with you. They don't change your original, perfect makeup. They were projections put into you by other people.

Secondly, now that you know this, it's up to you to uninstall this corrupt programming. Only you can return to the state in which you were meant to remain, which is the state of happiness.

But how?

First, let's dive into how we got here. One answer lies in the concept of attachment. As we grow, we have experiences. Some of those are traumatic. Our inexperienced brains fail to recognize those events as "wrong," so we normalize them, connect our identities to them, and allow them to define our lives. We then attach stories to these traumas—stories that shape our beliefs, our patterns, and our sense of self. Over time, those stories reinforce beliefs that may become limiting, causing us to live lives that do not align with our true potential.

Take, for example, the story I inherited from my childhood. I was born into an environment saturated with violence and fear. My father, a dangerously unpredictable alcoholic, was the source of most of that fear. My mother lived in constant terror, and my sister and I were raised with the understanding that our lives were always at risk. I found out later in life that even though my father often showed disdain for authority, he had applied to be in the military as well as an officer of the law. He was intelligent and physically capable, but he failed to pass his psychiatric examination when he admitted to torturing both animals and people. One of those people was me.

One of the most vivid memories of my childhood occurred on a hot summer evening when I was just a tiny three-year-old boy. My seven-year-old sister was sitting in a chair watching television when my father came into the room. As many fathers will, he began wrestling gently with me. As we played, I remember climbing onto him and laughing. At one point, he started becoming more aggressive in his movements. He was neither laughing nor smiling. I felt the energy of the moment shift. Even at that young age, I was familiar with this shift, and I immediately recognized the sudden change in his demeanor.

In one swift and fluid movement, he flipped me onto the ground, placing my entire body under him. This move was not at all difficult considering my toddler-sized stature and his six-foot-four-inch frame, which weighed 230 pounds.

To this day, I remember everything so vividly. His skin was warm and clammy on mine. The light through the sliding glass patio door turned into a thin horizon between his body and the living room carpet. I felt the warmth of the carpet pressing against my face while his body became heavier and heavier. I gasped for air, only able to fill my lungs with my own warm, recycled breath, which gave me no relief. I could not escape, I could not struggle, I could not breathe. Then, an eerie sense of calm overtook me, and I fell motionless.

My sister sat immobilized. I think about her perspective now–how, at just seven years old, she felt the same shift of our father's energy in the room. I think about how she struggled with feeling angry, power-less, and even fearful that something bad would happen to her next.

I don't remember coming to my senses. My sister says I cried, and my father mocked me for it. I only know that from that moment on, I held a new measure of fear. As the years passed, I cultivated a sense of empathy to help me navigate my father's moods and stay alive. I needed to stay hyper-aware of his state of mind and intentions. I had to feel the scale of danger he posed at any moment and be able to avoid him.

My mother was struggling to find her way with the tools she had available, and lived under a shroud of fear as well. When I was 14 years old, she left my father and took my sister and me with her. My sister set about building her own life, and eventually, my mother felt the best place for me would be away from her. This decision resulted in her leaving me in the care of a friend's mother. I was emotionally empty and felt as if I were broken and unlovable. These events, among many others, shaped my belief that I was not safe, not wanted, and that love would always lead to pain. I was convinced I was unworthy of love, and that I had to fight for my place in the world.

These beliefs stayed with me well into adulthood, influencing my actions and choices in ways I did not fully understand for a long time. Even after I escaped from my father's control, I subconsciously sought out danger and abandoned safe spaces. My most intimate relationships were marred by the belief that love always ends in abandonment. I had normalized trauma and danger and allowed it to define my reality.

Long into my adulthood, I paid a visit to the woman who took me in. She had been a single mother of three trying to make it on her own, as well.

"Why would you do that?" I asked her. "You had no obligation to me and had every right to refuse, call protective services, or any number of alternatives."

Her response was quick and clear: "I love you," she said.

I had not considered that the actions she took were purely out of love for me. I had not considered that I was lovable at all. That conversation allowed me to consider that my mother's motives were to find the best solution in a sea of poor options. She loved me. I realized that the only one who didn't love me was me!

I was finally able to let go of the belief that I was abandoned because I was unlovable. I rewrote it, instead, into the belief that my mother loved me enough to place me somewhere that would allow me to have a better life. That shift liberated me from the shackles of a toxic belief that had permeated every area of my life. I stepped into a new fate—one of love, empowerment, joy, service, and impact. This is now the reality I operate from and continually choose to create.

My traumas are unique; however, they are not special. We are all perfectly flawed. We all have moments we remember with pain, and we all attach beliefs to them. We all experience events that shape who we are.

Our logical brain uses input from our experiences to find patterns and move us forward in what it perceives to be the best possible way. This is fantastic in theory, but there are many pitfalls on this journey.

The trouble comes when our amygdala gets involved, which is the part of the brain that is designed for conflict. Our amygdala is wired to keep us safe and alive. Even when we are technically safe, if our brains interpret an event or emotion as dangerous, we are thrown into fear and survival mode. The brain can struggle to tell the difference between a nasty email and a saber-tooth tiger, meaning that most of us move through life unnecessarily ready for battle. This is especially tough for those of us who have experienced pain or trauma—and who hasn't? When the brain becomes more familiar with pain than with joy, it will automatically choose the familiar.

*This is who you are*, the brain says. *This is what you know. This is what life is.*

The survival mind sees familiarity as safe and has no interest in your expansion, your success, your joy, your sense of purpose, or your authentic values. It will always choose familiar discomfort over joyous unknowns, creating an internal battle between the change you desperately want and fear that the unknown is unsafe.

The key is learning to retrain the brain. To rewrite beliefs created by trauma, we must understand the distinction between events and traumas. Events are simply what happened in the past—the circumstances we have encountered, which are neutral and carry no inherent emotion. Trauma is activated when we attach emotions to life events and create stories around them. These stories shape our beliefs about ourselves and the world and can overshadow valuable lessons the events might offer.

For example, I created a story about my parents' actions without considering the challenges they faced. I allowed my emotionally charged beliefs to dictate my life until I finally recognized the truth: I was limiting myself by defining my identity through my past pain. When I saw this clearly, I began letting go of the stories and reclaiming the knowledge and growth hidden within the events.

My father was abusive. That is a fact. A fact about my father does not have to dictate my future. His actions caused me pain, but those actions define him, not me.

How many facts about others have you adopted as pieces of yourself? What stories can you let go of now that you are safer and wiser? What beliefs can you finally relinquish that you formed because of the actions of others that are completely unrelated to who you are?

Remember that the code programmed into each of us, starting at a young age, is an operating system coded with the virus of limiting beliefs. If you're unsure which code you're running, you can find an assessment at **www.drstaceykevinfrick.com/codecracker**.

Once you identify those faulty beliefs, you can do the vital work of removing this virus once and for all. And I hope you will. Pain is part of the human experience, but suffering is a choice.

# CHAPTER 2

# THE STATE OF SURVIVAL

---

*"Survival mode is supposed to be a phase that saves your life. It is not meant to be how you live."*

MICHELE ROSENTHAL

---

ON A WARM AUGUST EVENING IN 2019, TIMES SQUARE WAS ALIVE WITH its usual fusion of lights, street performers, and the hum of countless camera clicks and excited conversations. Suddenly, the deafening sound of gunshots cut through the joy.

*Pop! Pop! Pop!*

Time froze, but only for a moment. A two-second, shock-induced pause before chaos ensued.

People sprinted in every direction, some even knocking each other over. Some dodged into stores, others shed their shoes and purses, desperate to get away. Families were separated in the mayhem while sirens rang out over the shouting. Unfortunately, the realization that the sound came from a motorcycle that backfired, not a gun, came too late for the people who suffered injuries in the stampede.

This situation, now commonly referred to as Times Square Panic, is a perfect example of the fragility of calm in a world that has trained us for battle.

In the previous chapter, we discussed how our brains can declare war on us, but it's not the brain's fault. Life's constant demands, pressures, and challenges throw us into a perpetual state of survival. This survival reaction is more than a physical response; it is an emotional and psychological state where fear, anxiety, and stress dominate the mind. The emotional state of survival is characterized by a sense of scarcity, an underlying belief that we are not safe, or that there is not enough time, money, love, protection, or even opportunity.

When we operate from survival mode, our nervous system is locked into a "fight, flight, or freeze" response. This ancient mechanism, originally designed to protect us from immediate physical threats, now misfires in response to the pressures of modern life. Whether it is a looming deadline, financial worry, or relationship conflict, the body reacts as if under attack. In this state, higher reasoning and emotional processing are compromised, leaving us reacting out of fear instead of responding from a place of deductive reasoning or empowerment.

Emotionally, survival mode is exhausting. The body is constantly flooded with stress hormones like cortisol and adrenaline, which, over time, wear down our mental and emotional resilience. Instead of joy, creativity, and love, we feel constriction, anxiety, and often, isolation. The mind becomes hyper-focused on threats, whether real or perceived, and our emotional energy is spent on merely getting through the day.

When we are stuck in survival, we become reactive rather than proactive. Our decisions are shaped by fear, and this fear-driven mindset limits our potential. It closes us off from possibilities, innovation, and personal growth. The need to protect oneself overrides the ability to think expansively, which leads to stagnation both emotionally and in our external lives.

This emotional bracing keeps us on edge, and we are never fully able to relax or trust that things will be okay. We become hyper-vigilant, scanning for problems, and guarding ourselves against disappointment or pain, always bracing ourselves for the next challenge or setback.

Have you ever wondered why you snap at someone who might not deserve it? Why do you find yourself repeating the same patterns in relationships? How do certain bad habits continue to plague you year after year? Living in survival mode results in unconscious self-sabotaging behaviors because the emotional state of survival operates from a place of fear and distrust, even when there is no immediate danger. We might reject opportunities for growth, love, or abundance, simply because they challenge the comfort of what is familiar, even if that familiarity is steeped in pain.

Our patterns, no matter how dysfunctional or limiting, are perceived by our minds to be "manageable." This survival mechanism, deeply rooted in our evolutionary history, served our ancestors well in avoiding physical threats. In modern times, however, survival mode manifests as a resistance to change and growth, even a tendency to over-utilize our adrenaline when none whatsoever is needed.

When we consider stepping into new opportunities or unknown territory, even if that unknown territory is simply a sense of calm, our subconscious activates a primal defense system. It whispers warnings: "Stay here, where it's safe." The discomfort of uncertainty feels like danger, even when the stakes are as benign as learning a new skill, changing careers, opening up emotionally, or strolling through Times Square.

A subconscious that stays on high alert is a good thing when our lives are actually being threatened, but most of us are not in imminent danger. We just act like we are.

Many people who grew up in volatile, dysfunctional homes will even find themselves uncomfortable in stable relationships. They either find them boring or they assume that at any moment the calm will end, and then they sabotage it. Now they don't have to wait for the drama; they're causing it. In doing so, they maintain a false sense of security. They've restored the status quo in which their brains were conditioned.

## HOW THE STATE OF SURVIVAL PLAYS OUT IN DAILY LIFE

1. **Avoidance of Opportunities:** Growth opportunities often feel intimidating. You may rationalize turning them down, convincing yourself they're impractical or too risky, but this is often the subconscious working to keep you within the confines of the familiar.

2. **Repeating Old Patterns:** Despite wanting change, you may find yourself repeating behaviors or thought patterns that perpetuate the status quo. For example, you might avoid applying for a dream job, choosing instead to remain in a role that feels safe but unfulfilling.

3. **Overwhelming Self-Doubt:** The unknown often triggers a flood of self-doubt. Your subconscious mind might amplify thoughts like, "What if I fail?" or "I'm not good enough," creating a cycle of paralysis.

4. **Quickly Triggered:** When you are living on the edge, bracing for battle, and constantly seeking to protect yourself, you might assume that people are out to get you. This assumption can lead to a defensive nature that results in being easily triggered by the words and actions of others, even when there is no ill intent.

5. **Causing Trouble:** Maybe you cheat at work. Maybe you start fights with your partner. You don't do this consciously. Sadly,

your mind has become accustomed to things being difficult and painful. You expect things to fall apart. When everything is going smoothly, you can't even enjoy it because you are waiting for that inevitable moment when it all comes crashing down. The anticipation is too much, so you create the breakdown to avoid the shock of it coming unexpectedly.

## BREAKING THE CYCLE

1. **Recognize the Pattern:** Awareness is the first step to change. Notice when fear of the unknown is dictating your choices. Ask yourself, "Am I making this decision based on what feels familiar or what aligns with my true desires?"

2. **Create Small Wins:** Expansion doesn't have to be overwhelming. Take small, consistent steps into the unknown to recondition your subconscious to associate growth with safety. Each success, no matter how small, builds confidence and rewires your brain to accept the changes you want and need.

3. **Reframe Fear:** Instead of seeing fear as a stop sign, view it as a signal that you are moving toward growth. Feeling fear often means you are stepping into territory that has the potential to transform you. You must identify real fear from ambiguous fear to address it. If you cannot define the specific fear, you cannot address it; therefore, it is much like a mythical unicorn. It is real, but it does not exist.

4. **Commit to Self-Compassion:** Be kind to yourself as you navigate this process. The subconscious is not your enemy; it is trying to protect you. By showing yourself patience and

understanding, you create a nurturing space to move forward.

5. **Remind Yourself That You Are Safe:** Look where your feet are. You are not in a war zone. You are not in your past. You are not about to fight a saber-toothed tiger. Noticing where your feet are is a split-second way to remind yourself that in the present moment, right where you stand, all is well.

6. **Look for Evidence of Things Working Out:** Anytime you're feeling triggered or uncomfortable, and you're tempted to lash out or flee, try to remember a similar situation in which everything worked out fine. If you can't think of an example from your life, borrow evidence from someone else. Think of someone who has succeeded in a similar situation as proof that a positive outcome is possible.

The paradox of growth is that when we stay within *the known*, we limit our potential while stepping into *the unknown* expands it. The journey requires courage, persistence, and a willingness to face discomfort, but the rewards are immense. As you recondition your subconscious to see unfamiliar experiences as opportunities rather than threats, you unlock a life of possibility, fulfillment, and freedom. The more you work to cultivate calm in your life, the more likely it is that your brain will catch on and start working *for* you, not *against* you.

Calm and harmony might not be familiar, but that's all the more reason to embrace the unknown. It is not your enemy; it is your greatest ally in becoming the person you are meant to be.

# CHAPTER 3
# IDENTIFYING OLD ENERGY NARRATIVES

---

*"There is a voice that doesn't use words."*

RUMI

---

IMAGINE THAT YOU'VE JUST LEFT YOUR BUSY CORPORATE JOB FOR A weeklong vacation in the forest. You walk out of your office, suitcase in hand, and make your way through the crowded, noisy streets and into a taxicab. As you drive out of the city, you begin to exhale.

Once in the forest, you breathe in the clean air, feel your body decompress, and it's almost like the trees are speaking to you, not in words, but in vibrations. The Japanese call it "shinrin-yoku," which means "forest bath." At that moment, you are absorbing the ancient energetic imprint of the forest and allowing it to cleanse and renew you.

Now, imagine you leave the forest and drive to the ocean. Standing at the shoreline, you feel an inexplicable sense of fear. You know how to swim, yet the ocean's depth scares you. It's almost as if you have a memory of nearly drowning, even though it never happened to you.

At that moment, you might be experiencing cellular memory, which is, essentially, experiencing the energetic imprint of your ancestors. You inherited their eye color, why not their fears?

Next, you leave the ocean feeling out of sorts and head to a local restaurant. You walk through the doors and a smiling hostess greets you. She leads you to the back, where a group of servers is singing Happy Birthday to a dinner guest. The room is bright, the whole restaurant joins in, and pretty soon, you've forgotten about the unsettling waves of the ocean. Now you are carried along in this current of joy.

Why do these internal changes happen when your surroundings change?

Energy.

Everything is energy. It surrounds us, moves through us, and influences every moment of our lives. This concept of energy is not just a spiritual belief, but a scientific reality. Within the realm of science, energy is the fundamental force that powers everything in the universe. From the atoms that make up matter to the electromagnetic waves that transmit light, energy is the building block of all that exists. Physics teaches us that energy can neither be created nor destroyed; it only changes form.

In spirituality, many traditions acknowledge energy as the life force or vital essence that flows through all living things. Spiritual traditions might refer to this energy as "prana," "chi," or "spirit." Regardless of what you may call it, the invisible force that connects all beings and sustains life is widely experienced and undeniably powerful.

Despite the different terminology, the essence is the same. Whether viewed through a scientific or spiritual lens, energy is the fundamental substance of the universe. It is the invisible thread that weaves together the fabric of existence, and understanding this energy brings us closer to understanding the truth of both our physical and meta-physical realities.

Both science and spirituality point to the same conclusion: we have the power to influence our reality through our intentions. Whether through prayer, meditation, or focused thought, aligning our intentions with the universe's energy allows us to co-create our experience. By understanding the energetic nature of reality, we can harness this power to live more consciously and intentionally.

One of the most profound intersections of science and spirituality is the realm of healing. Spiritual traditions have long recognized the connection between the mind, body, and spirit, and many healing practices are based on the idea that imbalances in our energy can lead to physical and emotional illness.

In modern science, growing evidence supports the idea that our thoughts and emotions influence our physical health. Studies in the field of psychoneuroimmunology, for example, show that stress, anxiety, and negative emotions can weaken the immune system, while positive emotions and mindfulness practices promote healing.

Both science and spirituality acknowledge the role of energy in the healing process. Whether through practices like Reiki, acupuncture, or meditation, the goal is the same: to restore balance to the energy within us and promote well-being. This understanding of energy as the key to healing highlights the unity between scientific and spiritual approaches to health and wellness.

Additionally, science and spirituality lead us to the same conclusion: everything that exists is connected. Whether through the spiritual lens of unified consciousness or the scientific understanding of the interconnectedness of the quantum field, both perspectives point to the truth: that we are all part of a vast, energetic whole. Everything comes back to this energy that is always moving around us and through us. The key is to stay aware of the energy you absorb and hold onto.

Embracing the idea that everything is energy opens a doorway to a deeper understanding of the ways our environment impacts our behavior. We realize that much of what shapes our thoughts and actions stems from energies we absorbed long before we were aware of them.

Before birth, an energetic narrative is set into motion that defines who we are, what we should value, and our role in society. Our families, communities, and the institutions governing us reinforce this narrative. Over time, we internalize this story, believing it to be the truth about ourselves and our purpose in life. Throughout our lives, those we consider authoritative entities reinforce these energetic narratives. Religion, government, family, and society continuously bombard us with what our idea of success should be. If we are introspective and disregard their story of how we should behave, we risk being ostracized.

So, what happens when we outgrow this story we were given? When the narrative handed down to us no longer serves the present version of ourselves and conflicts with our authentic values and frequency, we start to feel uncomfortable, unfulfilled, and out of alignment.

In essence, our energy is off.

We become physically, mentally, and spiritually tired.

This inner conflict is a sign that we are not living a life that feels like our own. Instead, societal expectations, family pressures, or traumatic experiences have dictated our values and frequency.

I am always astounded by how many high-net-worth individuals who have achieved extraordinary success still struggle with self-esteem. The CEO of a multi-million-dollar company once told me that he never felt good enough and would lie in bed at night worrying that everything he built would come crashing down at any moment. After some digging, we concluded this was an old energetic narrative creeping into present thoughts.

His father, a harsh, disciplined man, repeatedly told him that he wasn't good enough. That message instilled in his son the belief that he would never live up to his father's expectations. Even as a 48-year-old man with all the evidence in the world that he could succeed, he had held onto the energy of his father's words and was waiting to fail.

We continued to dive deeper and explore his blocks. I knew him to be a good father and had heard as much from him, his wife, and all four of his children.

"If someone were to tell one of your children that they were not good enough, how would you respond?" I asked, "Would you let your child believe that, or would you show them a different reality where they were always good enough, and were becoming more so every day?"

"Of course!" he replied, stating that he would explain that those were someone else's beliefs and that they did not have to create their reality according to anyone but themselves. Yet he had let his father's projected energy echo in his mind and influence his thoughts and actions for decades! Once he realized he didn't want to keep it anymore, he could rewrite his own beliefs and step back into his own energy field, one of light, joy, and success.

When the narratives of our past and projected energies from others shape the reality in which we live, they foster the belief that life happens to us, rather than recognizing our role as creators of our own reality.

Even the goals we set are sometimes not our own. Many of us were taught that the worthiest of goals are what St. Thomas Aquinas described in the 13th century as idols (money, fame, pleasure, and power) are the worthiest of goals. This belief is constantly reinforced by the authoritative energies in our lives. Society, government, church, family, and work environments often espouse that the more you have of these idols, the more successful you are. This belief system completely dismisses the notion that we are all individuals with distinct, authentic values and energies. Success is specific to each of us. When you lead a life of service aligned with your authentic values, those idols become products of the way you live your life rather than goals. Following your true goals feels more fulfilling and impactful, but it also allows whatever rewards you enjoy to flow with abundance.

We can energetically change our narrative, and identify old energetic narratives that do not align or belong to us, and release them. We do this by cultivating a life that matches our own energetic frequency.

It's as simple as this: a person whose energetic frequency is one of calm, quiet serenity will never feel their best in a loud and frenzied environment. The noise and crowd will feel like an assault. On the other hand, a person who thrives in a busy, noisy environment may start to feel depressed in an environment that is too slow and quiet. If you absorb energies that misalign with your own, you will inevitably feel out of sync. That's why I make a point of constantly tuning in to the energy around me.

Years ago, I built several successful businesses and a multi-hospital system that grew exponentially. I was working 80-hour weeks, making a great deal of money, and enjoying the status that comes with being the "boss." One day, I woke up and realized that, while I had accomplished more than enough to prove myself, I wasn't happy. I felt validated by society's standards, but I wasn't happy. The energy was off. I had mistaken accomplishments for fulfillment.

What I craved was a quieter, simpler life. I sold the businesses, and I now spend my days doing work I love, exercising, and enjoying the outdoors. I no longer have the fancy title, but I have something more meaningful. I now have ownership of my energy.

When you commit to tuning in as a way of life, you learn to instantly detect frequencies that could pull you down so you can shift your path accordingly.

At what frequency do you thrive? What are you doing when you feel your best, most peaceful, and most alive? Where are you? Who is around you?

Now think about what you are doing when you feel down, insecure, and out of sorts. Humans tend to complicate things, but it really is quite simple to tune into your energy. Notice I didn't say it was *easy*, but it is *simple*.

The best way to feel better is to seek out people and environments that are an energetic match for you. When you do that, you will feel a sense of belonging, a sense of "home," which causes feelings of insecurity to melt away and reaffirms that your values and goals are worthy and valid.

I encourage you to become an expert in your own energy. Become an energetic warrior who fiercely protects your frequency.

Scientists have confirmed that everything is energy and energy is everything. And if energy is everything, the doorway to a life of fulfillment, joy, and purpose is always available to you.

# CHAPTER 4
# THE IMPACT OF
# NEGATIVE ENERGY

---

*"Be cautious with what you feed your mind and soul."*

STEVE MARABOLI

---

HAVE YOU EVER PAUSED TO CONSIDER THE WEIGHT OF YOUR WORDS? Not just the impact they have on others, but also how they resonate in the very fabric of the universe. Dr. Masaru Emoto, a Japanese scientist, dared to explore this question in his groundbreaking experiments examining the effect of words on water. His findings, though debated, sparked a wave of curiosity about the unseen power of language and intention.

Dr. Emoto's experiment was simple. He exposed water to various stimuli—spoken words, written phrases, music, and even silent intentions. The water samples were then frozen and examined under a microscope to observe the crystalline structures formed in the ice.

What he discovered was astonishing. When the water was exposed to words like "love" and "gratitude," or soothing music, it formed beautiful, symmetrical, and intricate crystals. On the other hand, water exposed to phrases like "you fool" or "I hate you" resulted in chaotic, fragmented, and disordered crystals.

Dr. Emoto's work suggests that words carry an energetic frequency that influences and affects the physical world. It's as though the water could "feel" the meaning of the words, reflecting harmony or discord accordingly. If negative energy has the power to affect objects and substances incapable of emotion, imagine what it can do to us.

Our bodies are composed of approximately sixty percent water. Emoto's research suggests a profound theory: the words we speak, the thoughts we entertain, and the energy we project could shape us on a cellular level.

Similar effects have been observed in other experiments with plants. Plants exposed to loving words thrive, while those subjected to neglect or harsh language wither. These findings echo the universal truth that what we absorb has a tangible impact on our experience of the world.

Negative energy can infiltrate our thoughts, emotions, and physical well-being, casting a shadow over our perceptions. We may not always notice its presence, but it influences the way we see ourselves and the world, creating barriers to happiness, fulfillment, and success.

Whether it comes from personal relationships, workplace dynamics, government institutions, or broader societal structures, negative energy finds its way into our lives through unspoken tensions, criticisms, and manipulations.

The most insidious thing about negative energy is the way it becomes normalized. We absorb it from our surroundings, internalize it, and continue to live under its influence. Over time, a state of mental fatigue, anxiety, and emotional distress becomes unavoidable.

Prolonged exposure to negativity shapes our worldview, convincing us that the world is a harsh, unforgiving place. It erodes our sense of optimism, creativity, and purpose.

Emotionally, negative energy creates a lack of inner harmony, resulting in feelings of frustration, anger, and resentment. Relationships become strained, and toxic environments drain our emotional vitality. Over time, these emotions accumulate, creating a heavy residue that affects future experiences and interactions. Much like being exposed to illness, negative energy clings to us until we consciously clear it.

Over time, we learn to expect disappointment and dysfunction, and, in doing so, attract more of it into our lives. Negative energy also impacts the physical body. Stress, a byproduct of constant exposure to negativity, manifests in countless ailments, including headaches, muscle tension, and even compromised immune systems.

Over time, as the body reacts physically to this energy by breaking down, our overall health suffers. Recognizing the presence of negative energy and its patterns in our lives is the first step toward reclaiming our mental, emotional, and physical well-being.

Have you ever wondered why nothing ever seems to work out? Or perhaps you have a string of bad luck and can't catch a break? The culprit could be negative energy.

If you are familiar with the Law of Attraction, you know that like attracts like. What that means is, if you have a flat tire and shortly after that get caught in a rainstorm, you may start saying things like, "This day is horrible." You are operating at a negative frequency. Since like attracts like, you attract additional negative experiences, which causes you to perpetuate the notion that the entire day is horrible.

Some people stay in this negative loop for years! Negative energetic narratives make us feel helpless and keep us stuck. Our ability to recognize these negative energies is a key component to self-empowerment, which is integral to protecting our positive frequency by avoiding negative ones.

Television might seem like a harmless activity, but violent shows, angry music, and persistent negative news coverage can wreak havoc on our subconscious. Distressing images can activate the amygdala and trick your brain into thinking you are being threatened, even if you are just sitting on your couch. You might suddenly start feeling anxious and have no idea why.

The more prolonged the exposure to negative energy, the more likely our brains will create neural pathways associated with stress and anxiety. Additionally, since humans are naturally empathic when we see someone being hurt on television, our mirror neurons fire, which causes our nervous systems to mimic the anguish we are witnessing.

I often hear people sharing that they feel sad, but can't quite put their finger on why. They are sometimes quick to label it as depression, and maybe it is. But perhaps it's as simple as being energetically aware. The odds are that they are not protecting their energy.

If we don't become our own energy warriors, we fail to construct boundaries that keep negativity from seeping in and pulling us down.

In her book, *Big Magic: Creative Living Beyond Fear,* Elizabeth Gilbert wrote, "I've never seen any life transformation that didn't begin with the person in question finally getting tired of their own bullshit."

It might sound crass, but it's a powerful point. One of the best ways to steel yourself against negativity is to become so tired of feeling unhappy that you'll do anything to protect yourself from negative energy. Getting tired of feeling terrible is a powerful motivator to do whatever it takes to set boundaries against threats to your frequency.

Focus on solutions, surround yourself with positive words and images, do something kind for others, and, as cliché as it sounds, find one thing to be thankful for every day. It's impossible to have a negative and a grateful thought at the same time. You attract what you project.

Don't believe me? Try it.

# CHAPTER 5
# THE WEIGHT OF HELPLESSNESS

---

*"What the caterpillar calls the end of the world, the master calls a butterfly."*

RICHARD BACH

---

THE WORD "HELPLESSNESS" IS DEFINED AS "THE INABILITY TO HELP oneself."

While I don't make a habit of contradicting the Merriam-Webster Dictionary, I need to amend that definition. Helplessness is actually the unwillingness to take back our power.

The ability to help ourselves is inherent in humanity. We all have it. What we don't all have is the knowledge of how to overcome our self-doubt and embody our sovereignty.

Martin E.P. Seligman coined the phrase "learned helplessness," which, he theorized, is a psychological state in which a person, after repeated exposure to uncontrollable events, believes they are powerless to change their situation. Essentially, when someone sees how bad things can get, we give up. If we adopt this theory, helplessness is not something we intrinsically are but rather something we learn.

Helplessness is the act of relinquishing control over our circumstances, emotions, or decisions to an external force, such as a person, situation, or belief. When we feel helpless, we perceive ourselves as incapable of affecting change, leaving our fate in the hands of others or external circumstances. This mental state may stem from past experiences, societal conditioning, or deeply rooted fears.

While it might seem like a passive state, helplessness is a transfer of power–an active choice. It is a weight that convinces us we have no control over our circumstances, leaving us to passively accept a life that does not align with our authentic values and desires.

At its core, when we surrender our agency to someone or something else, often unconsciously, we make an energetic transaction that can manifest in various ways:

1. **Seeking External Validation:** Relying on people or circumstances outside ourselves to determine our worth.

2. **Avoiding Responsibility:** Believing that outcomes are beyond our control absolves us of the need to take action.

3. **Adopting a Victim Mentality:** Blaming external factors instead of acknowledging our ability to influence our energy, and therefore, our situation.

This surrender might offer temporary relief from decision-making or accountability, but it comes at the cost of our autonomy, confidence, and potential for growth.

The effects of helplessness can be deeply pervasive, influencing various aspects of our emotional and social lives. Emotionally, helplessness can manifest as a form of paralysis, where feelings of anxiety, fear, and frustration dominate. This overwhelming sense of powerlessness creates a cycle of inaction and despair, making steps toward change feel difficult, if not impossible.

In relationships, helplessness can strain connections with others. Relying on loved ones or colleagues to solve our problems or validate our emotions creates unhealthy dynamics. This dependency can lead to frustration, resentment, or both for those we rely on and for ourselves when our expectations are inevitably unmet.

Helplessness also stunts personal growth. To avoid taking ownership of our choices is to limit the ability to learn, adapt, and develop resilience. Growth requires effort and agency, but a mindset of help-lessness denies us the opportunity to build confidence and expand our capabilities.

Finally, helplessness reinforces limiting beliefs. Each instance of feeling powerless adds to the narrative that we lack control. Breaking free from this mindset becomes increasingly difficult without a sense of autonomy.

The world we currently live in is no help. In this modern age, where technology amplifies every crisis and social media bombards us with carefully curated images of success, it is easy to feel like mere specta-tors in our own lives. The constant comparison to others, the societal pressure to achieve certain milestones, and the relentless flow of information all contribute to a sense of fear and inadequacy. Our own lives seem less significant, and we begin to doubt our ability to change anything.

Personal setbacks only reinforce this narrative. Financial struggles, health challenges, and unexpected losses all serve as reminders that the world is unpredictable and, at times, ruthless. This strains our resilience and, when fatigued, we give our power away to try and relieve the stress placed on us, not realizing that it is contributing to the problem and not the solution.

The cure for helplessness is embracing our power, acknowledging our ability to influence our lives, and trusting in our capacity to grow.

Reclaiming this power is not just about changing outcomes; it is about rediscovering who we are and stepping boldly into the fullness of our potential.

## THE PATH BACK TO EMPOWERMENT

Breaking free from helplessness requires reclaiming the power we have given away. Here is how:

1. **Recognize the Pattern:** The first step is identifying where and why we feel helpless. Reflect on situations where you have relinquished control and consider what beliefs or fears underlie these actions.

2. **Shift Your Perspective:** Reframe challenges as opportunities to exert influence, no matter how small. Instead of saying, "I can't do anything about this," ask, "What's one thing I *can* do?"

3. **Take Small, Intentional Actions:** Building a sense of control starts with small victories. Each step forward—no matter how minor—challenges the narrative of helplessness and reinforces your capacity to effect change.

4. **Cultivate Internal Validation:** Shift your focus from seeking approval or solutions externally to building confidence and trust in your own abilities. Practices like journaling, mindfulness, and self-reflection can strengthen your internal sense of worth.

5. **Set Boundaries:** Helplessness often thrives when we are overly influenced by others' opinions or demands. Establishing boundaries protects your energy and reinforces your autonomy.

When we reclaim the power we have given away, the effects are transformative. We become more confident, our relationships become healthier and more balanced, and we unlock our potential for growth, creativity, and fulfillment.

The narrative of helplessness is a lie.

It is a story designed to keep us trapped in fear and prevent us from embracing the power of free will and personal responsibility. The world would have us believe that we must conform to its expectations, even if they do not align with our truth. It convinces us to settle for a life that feels inauthentic, one driven by external pressures rather than internal purposes.

Helplessness is not our destiny—it is a story we've been taught to believe. The truth is that our power has never left us; it waits patiently for us to reclaim it. The moment we recognize that we are not victims of circumstance but creators of our reality, we step into the fullness of our potential.

Liberation begins with the simple, profound choice to say, "I will no longer surrender my power." In that choice lies the transformation from caterpillar to butterfly, from despair to sovereignty, from helplessness to hope.

# CHAPTER 6

# REDEFINING WEALTH

---

*"True wealth comes less from having riches than from knowing how to live richly."*

ERIC MICHAEL LEVENTHAL

---

FOR MANY OF US, WEALTH IS DEFINED BY MATERIAL SUCCESS—MONEY, possessions, station in society, fame. But what if true wealth is something else entirely? Throughout my life, I have been a veterinarian, a business owner, an investor, and an inventor, among other things. I have pursued many different ventures, and I have found that the ones that brought me true fulfillment were not those focused on financial gain or recognition. Instead, they were the ones driven by service, joy, and curiosity.

Now that's not to say that financial security isn't important. It is. However, when I defined wealth solely in terms of money or status, the venture often failed or at least did not perform to my expectations and desires. When, on the other hand, I approached the work intending to align with my authentic values and serve others, I found meaning, joy, and deep satisfaction. My true wealth was not the financial reward, but the fulfillment that came from aligning with a purpose greater than myself.

The gift I discovered while practicing medicine as a veterinarian was that the service was the goal. I always loved science and animals, and I remember the excitement and joy I felt when I finally started practicing. I remember saying the words out loud, "I can't believe I actually get to do this." I felt as if I did not need to eat, sleep, take breaks, or allocate energy anywhere else to feel fulfilled. The joy of this alignment was the core of my success. This energetic abundance was wealth. I was able to heal the sick and enrich the lives of those who cared for them. No amount of money, fame, power, or pleasure would fill that space. My discomfort only began when I felt the pressure of the old energetic narratives pushing me to seek more. Over time, when I entangled the idols into my service and made them goals, the light of my joy dulled. At the time, I did not have the emotional intelligence or the tools to understand what was happening.

I will never forget one particular conversation with a dear friend. This friend and her husband are high-net-worth individuals, showing all the spoils of their financial prowess. They have a life many would aspire to. I had reached the same status, and I remember her looking at me with complete authenticity and saying, "Wow, congratulations! You have arrived!"

Her words made me feel empty and even invoked more discomfort. I did not feel like I had arrived. I could only see the accomplishments that she saw and could not feel any sense of fulfillment or impact from them.

I could not even muster any expression on my face when I replied in all sincerity, "I haven't done anything." I was not connected fully with my service, only my status. I could not allow myself to feel that I was making an impact in the world and that the impact *was* my wealth.

I tried to cure my discomfort with the things others told me would help, but eventually, I left medicine altogether. No matter how much service I could put into the world, I felt as though it was not enough. When the goal shifted to things like making more money and getting more clients, numbers trumped my heart. Hitting those benchmarks took priority, and when the numbers fell short, I felt a sense of failure kick in. I became exhausted.

I was measuring success with the wrong barometer, focused on old energetic wealth and not the wealth that aligned with my authentic values. It is difficult to speculate; however, I have wondered if I had been able to realign with my authentic values and establish boundaries around them, maybe I would still be practicing medicine today.

Wealth is not about what we possess, but about how we feel and how deeply we live in alignment with our purpose. It is about recognizing the wealth that comes from within, the energy that drives us forward, and the connections we forge along the way.

In the chapters ahead, we will explore how to harness, cultivate, and sustain this energy, shaping not only our individual lives but also the collective human experience. As we continue to identify and embrace our true potential and value, we step into a life that feels more vibrant, authentic, and aligned with the true essence of who we are.

The key to breaking free from the limiting narrative that money equals success is to first recognize that it exists. What beliefs have you attached to yourself that no longer serve you? What patterns are you repeating out of familiarity rather than authenticity? Whose goals are you trying to achieve? Who is setting the bar? Your parents? Your friends? Once you identify these limiting beliefs and their sources, you can begin to release them and write your own narrative.

Living a life of true fulfillment requires integrity—honoring your values, desires, and truths, rather than conforming to the expectations of others. This journey of self-discovery requires courage, honesty, and a willingness to face the unknown. Yes, you need money to pay your bills, but just for a moment, imagine that everything was free and everyone was equal. In this scenario, money becomes irrelevant because everyone has the same amount and no more is needed.

How would you live? What would you do? What would you let go?

The quest for validation is a deeply ingrained human trait. We often find ourselves caught in the cycle of either proving our worth, ideas, or competence to others or improving aspects of our lives for personal growth. While both of these approaches may seem similar on the surface, they originate from fundamentally different mindsets and have vastly different impacts on our lives. Understanding this distinction is crucial for those seeking fulfillment and authenticity.

## THE SOCIAL ASPECT OF PROVING

Proving is intrinsically tied to societal norms and expectations. For example, a student might aim to prove their intelligence by acing exams, not necessarily to learn, but to earn respect or approval. Similarly, professionals might overwork to prove their dedication, driven by the fear of appearing lazy or incompetent.

Proving something inherently involves an external audience. It stems from the desire to demonstrate worth, correctness, or superiority. Whether it is proving our skills to a boss, proving our knowledge in an argument, or proving our worth in relationships, the act is fueled by an external focus.

This external orientation can become exhausting. It is akin to chasing a moving target: what satisfies one person or audience might not impress another. Thus, proving often leads to a cycle of perpetual striving, with fleeting moments of satisfaction.

Characteristics of proving:

1. **Your feelings are dependent on others:** Proving requires an external observer to validate the effort. The measure of success lies outside yourself.

2. **It is ego-driven:** Often, the need to prove stems from insecurity or fear of being judged. It is a defense mechanism to shield against perceived inadequacies. You feel better about yourself when someone compliments your achievements.

3. **You have finite goals:** Once a point is proven, the task ends. It is not about continuous growth but about reaching a momentary state of recognition.

4. **You feel performance pressure:** The need to prove often brings anxiety. "What if I fail?" becomes a recurring question, and the need to succeed steals the joy from the journey.

## THE PERSONAL ASPECT OF IMPROVING

Improving liberates you from the need to conform to external standards. For example, a person might work on their fitness not to look good for others but to feel healthier and more energetic. In this paradigm, the joy comes from seeing tangible progress and feeling a sense of accomplishment that is independent of others' opinions.

Improving, in contrast, is an internal process that is about becoming better for your own sake, without concern for external validation. When you focus on improvement, you set your own benchmarks and measure success based on your desire for personal growth rather than societal approval.

Characteristics of Improving:

1. **You are self-driven:** Improvement is intrinsically motivated. It is about aligning with your values, goals, and aspirations.

2. **You have infinite goals:** Unlike proving, improvement has no endpoint. It is a lifelong journey of learning, adapting, and evolving.

3. **You feel minimal pressure:** Since the focus is on progress, not perfection, improvement feels more empowering and less stressful.

4. **You feel empowered through action:** When improving, you are in control. You dictate the pace, scope, and direction of your efforts.

## THE PSYCHOLOGICAL DICHOTOMY

The difference between proving and improving ultimately lies in whom you are accountable to. When proving, the accountability is external. You are answerable to others—their opinions, judgments, and standards. In improving, the accountability is internal. You answer only to yourself and strive to meet your own expectations.

This distinction affects how we perceive challenges and failures. For instance, in proving, failure is seen as a blow to your identity. It reinforces fears of inadequacy. In improving, failure is reframed as a stepping stone. It is an opportunity to learn and grow.

Transitioning from a proving mindset to an improving mindset requires conscious effort. Here are a few key strategies you can try:

1. **Identify your motivations.**
   - Ask yourself: "Am I doing this to seek approval, or because it aligns with my values?"
   - EXAMPLE: Instead of taking on extra work to impress your

boss, focus on tasks that help you develop skills you care about.

2. **Reframe success.**
   - Shift from external benchmarks to internal ones.
   - EXAMPLE: Celebrate completing a workout because you are building discipline, not because you are chasing compliments.

3. **Practice Self-Compassion**
   - Allow yourself room to grow without judgment.
   - EXAMPLE: If you stumble while learning a new skill, focus on the progress you've made rather than the mistakes.

4. **Limit Social Comparisons**
   - Reduce your exposure to environments that fuel comparison, such as social media.
   - EXAMPLE: Instead of comparing your progress to others, track your personal growth journey.

While improving is the healthier mindset, proving is not inherently bad. In some cases, the need to prove can act as a catalyst for improvement. For instance, wanting to prove your competence in a new job might motivate you to acquire new skills. However, the key is ensuring that proving does not overshadow your personal growth goals.

When you choose to improve rather than prove, you reclaim your power. You are no longer at the mercy of external opinions and judgments. Instead, you create a life that is aligned with your values and aspirations. This shift not only fosters genuine growth but also nurtures inner peace, confidence, and fulfillment. By focusing on improving, you are free to define success on your own terms—a freedom that no amount of proving can offer.

So, ask yourself: What is your definition of wealth, and does it align with your authentic values? What motivates you to pursue your goals? Is it a desire for external validation, or is it a deep calling to serve others and make a difference? Where do you feel you are trying to "improve" something, and where are you trying to "prove" something? What feels like a privilege to do? When we redefine wealth as a journey of service and personal growth rather than a destination of material success, we open ourselves up to a life of true abundance.

# CHAPTER 7

# SETTLE, DON'T SETTLE

---

*"When you settle for crumbs, you will always be starving."*

UNKNOWN

---

IN THE EARLY 1970S, STRUGGLING ARTISTS SEEMED TO POPULATE EVERY street corner in New York City. One such artist in particular was at rock bottom. With no income and no offers, he was forced to sleep in the bus terminal for several nights and even sold his beloved dog for $50 just to afford food—a heart-wrenching decision that underscored the depths of his desperation. The only thing that kept him going was a refusal to settle for this being the end of his story.

He had a dream, and he had a screenplay he had written, which he was sure would become a hit. He began pounding on doors and shopping the script to production studios, but he faced rejection after rejection. Finally, a studio offered him $125,000 for the screenplay—a small fortune for someone who was totally broke–but there was a catch. They didn't want him to act in the movie.

For him, playing the main character was non-negotiable. He saw himself in the character. To him, selling the script and letting someone else play the part would be the ultimate act of settling. He turned the offer down.

Then a higher bid came in: $250,000. Again, he said no. Finally, they offered $350,000. Imagine the temptation—a struggling actor, barely scraping by, declining enough money that would change his life forever. But he held firm. He was determined not just to *sell* a story, but to *live* it.

Eventually, the studio agreed to let him star in the film, and when it was released, it became a cultural phenomenon. That writer and actor was Sylvester Stallone, and that movie was Rocky.

The real triumph wasn't the film's success—it was Stallone's refusal to settle. If he had sold the script and walked away, he might have become financially secure, but he would have abandoned the dream that defined him.

Settling for less may provide short-term relief, but it robs us of the opportunity to achieve something extraordinary—settling into the life we are meant to live.

The world is full of compromises and quick fixes, but greatness belongs to those who hold out for what truly aligns with their vision, even when the odds are stacked against them.

In the journey of self-empowerment and personal growth, there is a crucial distinction between *settling into* your life and *settling for* it. The difference may seem subtle, but they represent fundamentally different mindsets and approaches to life that can profoundly impact how you navigate challenges, set goals, and achieve fulfillment.

## SETTLING FOR: THE VOICE OF LIMITATION

When you *settle for* something, you accept less than what you desire, deserve, or are capable of achieving. This mindset often stems from fear, doubt, or societal conditioning.

*Settling for* says:

- "This is as good as it gets."
- "I should be grateful for what I have, even if it doesn't feel right."
- "Dreams are for others, not for me."

*Settling for* **something can manifest in various areas of life, such as:**

- Staying in an unfulfilling job because you fear change.
- Remaining in a relationship that lacks joy or growth out of fear of being alone.
- Ignoring your dreams because pursuing them feels risky or impractical.

While settling for something may bring short-term comfort, it leads to long-term dissatisfaction, resentment, and a sense of being disconnected from your true self.

## SETTLING INTO: THE ENERGY OF ALIGNMENT

By contrast, when you *settle into* something, you embrace it with intention, awareness, and trust. *Settling into* your life means aligning with your authentic values and purpose, even if the path forward is uncertain or challenging.

*Settling into* says:

- "I trust where I am right now, and I'm open to growth and possibility."

- "I will embrace the present moment while working toward my goals."
- "I deserve a life of joy and fulfillment, and I am willing to create it and wait for it if necessary."

*Settling into* **your life involves:**

- Accepting the present moment as a foundation for growth rather than as a final destination.
- Trusting your journey and acknowledging that every experience has value.
- Taking intentional steps toward your authentic goals, even when progress feels slow.

This approach fosters a mindset of empowerment, resilience, and gratitude. It allows you to appreciate where you are while maintaining a clear vision of where you want to go.

## The Key Differences

| SETTLING FOR | SETTLING INTO |
|---|---|
| Operates from fear and scarcity | Operates from trust and abundance |
| Feels like a compromise | Feels like alignment |
| Ignores or suppresses your values | Embraces and aligns with your values |
| Creates resentment and stagnation | Promotes gratitude and growth |
| Focuses on external validation | Focuses on inner fulfillment |

## WHY DO WE *SETTLE FOR?*

There are many reasons why people settle for less than they deserve:

1. **Fear of the Unknown:** The comfort of familiarity can outweigh the uncertainty of pursuing something greater.

2. **Conditioning:** Societal and cultural norms may pressure individuals to conform rather than thrive.

3. **Self-Doubt:** A lack of belief in your abilities can make big dreams feel out of reach.

4. **Misaligned Priorities:** Focusing on what others expect instead of what truly matters to you.

Understanding these drivers is the first step toward breaking free from the habit of settling for.

## HOW TO SHIFT FROM SETTLING FOR TO SETTLING INTO

1. **Reflect on Your Current Reality:**
   - What areas of your life feel misaligned or unfulfilling?
   - Are you accepting less than what you desire or deserve?

2. **Revisit Your Authentic Values:**
   - Define what truly matters to you.
   - Evaluate whether your current choices reflect these values.

3. **Embrace the Present Moment:**
   - Accept where you are as a starting point, not an endpoint.

- Practice gratitude for what you have while maintaining a vision for more.

4. **Take Small, Aligned Actions:**
   - Identify one step you can take to align your life with your authentic values.
   - Celebrate progress, no matter how small.

5. **Cultivate a Mindset of Trust:**
   - Trust that your journey is unfolding as it should.
   - Release the fear of failure and embrace the growth that comes with taking risks.

### A PRACTICAL EXAMPLE: CAREER CHOICES

Imagine you are in a job that pays the bills but leaves you feeling drained and uninspired.

Settling for this job might look like telling yourself:

- "At least I have a job."
- "I don't have the skills to do anything else."

Settling into your current role, however, would involve acknowledging it as a stepping stone:

- "This job provides financial stability while I explore other opportunities."
- "I am gaining valuable experience that will support my future goals."

From this perspective, you can take proactive steps, such as upskilling, networking, or creating a timeline for transitioning to a more fulfilling role.

## THE POWER OF CHOOSING TO SETTLE INTO YOUR LIFE

When you settle *into* your life, you reclaim your power. You acknowledge that, while you may not be exactly where you want to be, you are not stuck. Every moment becomes an opportunity to learn, grow, and align more closely with your authentic self.

Am I asking you to give up on a dream? Maybe. If that dream does not serve you, is fueled by the expectations of others, and robs you allow your fulfillment, then yes. If this is the case, it is almost certainly someone else's dream that you have told yourself should be yours.

By settling into life rather than settling for it, you open the door to endless possibilities. You honor your worth, embrace your journey, and trust that the best is yet to come. None of us is Sylvester Stallone, but we are all writing the scripts of our lives; scripts in which we are the main characters. It's up to us to write and direct every scene, to stand up for our choices, to choose our supporting cast, to add in plot twists when things get dry, and ultimately, to bring our stories full circle into conclusions that inspire us.

This mindset shift is not just a change in perspective—it is a transformation in how you live, love, and lead your life.

# CHAPTER 8
# IDENTIFYING AUTHENTIC VALUES

---

*"The first secret of getting what you want, is knowing what you want."*

ARTHUR HLAVATY

---

HOW DO YOU KNOW IF YOU'RE SETTLING FOR LESS IN LIFE WHEN YOU don't even know what "more" means to you? It's like wandering through a forest without a compass—every path looks like it might lead somewhere, but you never know if it's where you truly want to go.

Sylvester Stallone knew what his "more" was. The studios assumed his "more" meant more money, but he had a different set of values. His "more" was playing the lead role. If he wasn't clear on his authentic values, he may have accepted the big paycheck, stayed in the background, and none of us would know his name today.

The truth is, you can't know if you're settling if you don't know what you're striving for. And you won't know what to strive for until you're clear on what truly matters to you. That's where your values come in —not the ones society imposes on you, or the ones you've inherited without question, but the authentic values that resonate with the deepest parts of who you are.

Your values are the foundation of a meaningful life. They're not just guiding principles; they're the lens through which you see the world and decide what's worth your time, energy, and love. Without knowing them, you risk living by someone else's blueprint, building a life that doesn't fit your soul.

So, how do you uncover your authentic values? How do you separate what truly matters to you from the noise of what you think should matter? It begins with asking hard questions and being brave enough to sit with the answers.

We explored the dangerous trap of the idols—wealth, fame, and other surface-level achievements that stand only to impress others. True wealth flows when we manifest a reality that harmonizes with our integrity and purpose. It is the richness that arises when our actions, values, and inner truths align, creating a sense of fulfillment that surpasses the temporary satisfaction of external achievements. It is a system by which we can identify the root of our discomfort, release ourselves from limiting beliefs, and create a reality of impact, fulfillment, and joy.

Purpose, service, and intention need to align with your authentic values in order to provide balance, and harmony to the form in which we apply energy and channel our efforts. In this way, we can free ourselves from what is not ours and is not serving us, execute our service in excellence, knowing that we are committed to the intention, and allow only challenges delivered in grace instead of difficulty and frustration.

When faced with challenges or aspirations, we often focus on the "how" — the steps we need to take, the strategies to employ, and the practicalities of achieving our goals. While the "how" is undeniably important, it is the "what" and the "why" that truly lead to lasting transformation and fulfillment. These two questions dig deeper into our core values, motivations, and purpose, offering clarity and direction in ways that the "how" alone never can.

Asking ourselves "what" and "why" is far more transformative and empowering than focusing solely on "how." By shifting our mindset and allowing ourselves to dive into these deeper inquiries, we can tap into a wellspring of authentic motivation and intention, making the path forward clearer and more aligned with who we truly are.

The question "What?" grounds us in a vision of what we genuinely want. It requires us to get specific about our desires, goals, and outcomes. When we ask ourselves, "What do I really want?" we begin to paint a picture of what success, happiness, or fulfillment looks like for us individually. This clarity is crucial because it serves as a compass for every action we take.

Without first defining our "what," it is easy to get lost in a sea of external pressures, expectations, and vague goals. We might pursue careers, relationships, or paths that we think we "should" be on, only to find ourselves feeling unfulfilled because we never asked what we truly wanted.

By starting with "what," we root our actions in a clear vision. Knowing what we are striving for allows us to shape our decisions and efforts with intention, ensuring that every step we take is meaningful and aligned with our authentic desires.

While "what" defines our vision, "why" uncovers the motivation behind it. This question requires us to dig into the core of why our desires and goals matter to us. It invites us to reflect on what is profoundly important and valuable in our lives. When we know our "why," we tap into the emotional and energetic fuel that sustains us through obstacles, uncertainties, and setbacks.

Without asking "why," we risk pursuing goals that do not fit us. We might chase after achievements or status because we have been conditioned to think they are important, but unless those goals resonate deeply with our values, we will struggle to stay motivated. The "why" provides the emotional connection we need to stay committed even when the journey gets difficult.

For example, if someone asks, "Why do I want to start my own business?" and the answer is "Because I want freedom, creativity, and to help others," then that person's motivation is rooted in personal empowerment and contribution. This "why" gives them the resilience and clarity needed to push forward, even when the road is tough. Without that deep motivation, it becomes much easier to give up at the first sign of difficulty.

While the "how" is practical and tactical, it becomes meaningless without the foundation of the "what" and "why." Knowing how to do something without understanding what you want or why you want it leads to a hollow pursuit. You might accomplish tasks, reach goals, and check off to-do lists, but without a clear sense of purpose, these achievements can feel empty.

The "how" can only take you so far. It may get you through short-term objectives, but when challenges arise or when the excitement of novelty fades, the "how" alone cannot sustain you. This is where many people struggle—they become focused on the mechanics of achieving something without anchoring their actions in deeper meaning. When we focus on the "how," we limit the form by which our deepest desires can manifest by energetically restricting ourselves. Letting go of the "how" to focus on the "what" and "why" releases these limitations, opening a cornucopia of possibilities.

When you first define your "what" and "why," the "how" becomes much more intuitive. It flows naturally from your vision and purpose, allowing you to align with actions that feel authentic and meaningful. Instead of trying to force solutions, you are guided by a deeper clarity that makes the "how" feel less like a puzzle to solve and more like a process of unfolding.

When we ask, "What do I truly want?" we might realize that the goals we have been chasing are not actually our own but are influenced by society, family, or external pressures. When we go further and ask ourselves, "Why is this important to me?" we uncover the values, beliefs, and experiences that drive us.

To truly experience the transformative power of "what" and "why," we need to make self-inquiry a regular practice. This means integrating these questions into our everyday decision-making processes. Instead of jumping straight to "how," pause and ask yourself:

- "What do I truly want in this situation?"
- "Why is this important to me?"
- "What will this decision or action contribute to my overall sense of fulfillment?"

By consistently asking these questions, we cultivate greater clarity and purpose in our lives. We begin to live more intentionally, choosing actions and paths that are aligned with our true desires and values rather than reacting to external pressures or default patterns.

Your authentic values should resonate with you as absolute truths. Wavering from those truths should produce an uncomfortable physical feeling. Think back to when you were a kid and someone talked you into something wrong. You may have gone along with it, but the awareness that you were acting out of alignment with your values nagged at you the whole time. And when your parents found out, maybe you felt a little sick to your stomach? Your body knows when your mind has led you astray. Your heart knows when you have betrayed your own deepest desires. Your soul knows when you have compromised on your "more".

In life's journey, living in alignment with your authentic values and integrity is like holding a compass that guides you toward a purposeful, authentic existence. To live in alignment means to bridge the gap between what you believe and how you behave, leading to a life of coherence and fulfillment.

Once we identify and align with our authentic values, we can then place a round peg in a round hole. The correct action can be taken, and we can move forward to create impactful, fulfilling solutions.

# CHAPTER 9

# HOW YOUR BRAIN MISBEHAVES
## & WHAT TO DO ABOUT IT

---

*"You're learning to be nourished by the love you give, not by the validation offered in response to your giving."*

MATTHEW KAHN

---

WE LIKE TO THINK OF OURSELVES AS INDEPENDENT THINKERS. WE PRIDE ourselves on our ability to make our own decisions. From the time we are children, we wear our independence like a defiant badge of honor.

"You're not the boss of me!"

"I can do it myself."

"Don't tell me what to do!"

But beneath this veneer of autonomy lies a powerful, often subconscious, force that most of us carry into adulthood: the need for validation.

This need to see our beliefs affirmed and our choices approved of shapes the way we perceive reality. It's not just a quirk of human nature; it's a survival mechanism, etched deep into our psyche. We're drawn to environments, relationships, and information that make us feel seen and understood. It's comforting, almost addictive, to live in a world that agrees with us.

Enter the algorithms. Nowhere is this phenomenon more apparent than in the world of social media. Facebook, Instagram, YouTube, and their digital counterparts have perfected the art of feeding our hunger for validation. Engage with a post about your political views, and you'll see more of the same. Click on a video about your favorite conspiracy theory and get ready for an endless stream of content that reinforces that theory. The algorithms don't have an agenda. They simply optimize for engagement, and what engages us most is whatever makes us feel right.

This reality is not limited to social media. It permeates every aspect of our lives. From the news we consume to the friends we keep, we're building a house of mirrors where every reflection affirms, "You're right. You're on the right path. Keep going."

But is this validation always a gift? Or can it be a trap? To understand its power, we need to confront the uncomfortable truth: seeking validation is as much about reinforcing our sense of identity as it is about avoiding the discomfort of doubt.

How can we recognize when we're being manipulated by this seductive need? And how can we reclaim the courage to stand for our own convictions, whether anyone approves of them or not?

It starts with understanding why this happens. The human mind is a masterful architect, constantly constructing a reality that aligns with our deeply held beliefs, whether they are empowering or limiting. Understanding this process can unlock powerful opportunities for personal growth, decision-making, and emotional resilience.

At the core of this phenomenon is a psychological process known as confirmation bias. This term describes our tendency to search for, interpret, and remember information in a way that confirms our existing beliefs while ignoring or downplaying evidence that contradicts them. Our brain does this automatically.

The brain operates through neural networks—pathways strengthened by repeated thoughts and behaviors. When a belief is formed, it is encoded in these networks. Over time, the brain becomes adept at recognizing patterns and filtering information that reinforces these beliefs.

When we encounter information that aligns with our beliefs, the brain releases dopamine, reinforcing the "rightness" of our perspective.

When we encounter evidence that challenges our beliefs, the brain experiences discomfort known as cognitive dissonance. To resolve this tension, we often rationalize or dismiss the conflicting information. We seek evidence of our "correctness", and this plays out in countless ways in our everyday lives:

- **In relationships,** if you believe a partner is untrustworthy, you are more likely to notice behaviors that align with that belief, even if they are minor or ambiguous. Most people these days take their phones into the bathroom. When your partner takes his or her phone into the bathroom, however, you might assume they are hiding something.

- **In career development,** the belief that you are not "good enough" may lead you to overlook successes and focus disproportionately on setbacks. You may find yourself with great ideas, yet remain silent during meetings. Why would they listen to you anyway?

- **In personal contexts,** you may believe that you will never lose weight, so you allow yourself to eat poorly and surround yourself with friends who say things like, "Life is short, eat cake!"

I remember vividly a time when I was in a relationship with someone for whom I cared very much. Gradually, as the relationship progressed, I started noticing that there were occasions where they seemed critical of me for what I considered minor faults. In time, criticism progressed into verbal and even physical abuse.

I sought out counseling to help guide us through the relationship and understand more clearly all the dynamics involved. I remember quite clearly being told by both my partner and the therapist that they wanted me to explain my emotions verbally, even offering me the emotion wheel as a guide to help me verbalize my feelings. I thought I was doing a good job with this, but I didn't know what I didn't know, right?

One day, during therapy, I was explaining my feelings by using the emotion wheel as they had requested. I did a deep dive into what I felt was influencing my emotions and the feelings surrounding them. I felt it to be cathartic and a thorough explanation backed by sincerity and vulnerability. What happened next left my jaw on the floor. The therapist looked me in the face and said, "I really need you to express your feelings so we can see that you really understand where we are coming from."

I was so confused. I realized in that instant that I had built a team of people around me that confirmed the lack of self-worth that had become so familiar to me. My mind had instructed my reality to create a confirmation bias against my empowerment, so I surrounded myself with people who would gaslight me and take whatever power I was willing to hand over to them.

At that moment, I understood clearly *what* was going on, but I had no idea *why*. I felt a mix of gratitude at my revelation and self-loathing that I put myself in that position.

When I explained this situation to a dear friend, he said to me, "You don't have to put up with that."

That one sentence helped me realize that the only relevant questions I needed to answer were: *What can I learn from this? How do I want to feel? What actions can I take to move closer to the way I want to feel?*

I began writing a new confirmation bias based on an elevated minimum acceptable standard for the way I would allow anyone in my life to treat me.

Belief validation is a double-edged sword. When it helps, it reinforces cultural norms, allows for fast decision-making, and boosts confidence by validating self-worth. Yet, when it hurts, it perpetuates negative self-belief, causes us to resist growth, and limits our expansion by pulling us into the trap of groupthink. How, then, do we reprogram our brains to release the need for validation?

Awareness of this mental process is the first step toward harnessing its power rather than being controlled by it. Here is how you can shift the way your brain validates beliefs:

1. **Challenge Automatic Thoughts:** When you catch yourself clinging to a belief, ask: *What evidence supports this? What evidence contradicts it?*

   Practice viewing situations from multiple perspectives. Let's say you're at a restaurant and the waitress isn't friendly. Your belief system might immediately be triggered to the point that you take her coldness personally.

   "She is being rude to me," you might think. What if, however, she is dealing with a difficult situation at home that is weighing on her heart?

   Choosing to challenge the trigger beliefs is a huge step towards peace as it stops the tendency to take things personally and activates empathy.

2. **Expose Yourself to Diverse Information:** Seek out viewpoints and experiences that challenge your assumptions. Engaging with different perspectives can weaken rigid beliefs and create space for growth. If someone disagrees with your political views or the way you handled a situation, get curious! Allow them to explain their point of view and see what you can learn from it.

3. **Reinforce Empowering Beliefs:** Use affirmations and visualization to strengthen beliefs that align with your goals. The brain responds to repetition, so consistent focus on positive beliefs can reshape neural pathways over time.

4. **Practice Mindfulness:**Mindfulness helps us observe our thoughts without judgment, creating a gap between stimulus and response. This practice can reduce the automatic validation of unhelpful beliefs.

## A CALL TO AWARENESS

Your beliefs shape your reality, but they are not immutable. When we understand how our brain seeks proof to validate them, we can take control of the process, shedding limiting narratives and building empowering ones. This transformation does not happen overnight, but with practice and patience, you can align your beliefs with the life you truly desire.

The next time you are faced with a challenging thought or situation, remember that your brain is doing its job—protecting you by confirming what you have always believed to be true. But you have to do your job too- exercise the power to decide whether those beliefs serve you or hold you back. That decision in itself can change everything.

# CHAPTER 10
# FLIPPING THE SWITCH
## UNVEILING POSITIVE ENERGY

---

*"Positive energy is contagious. Negative energy is also contagious. Only you can choose which you carry and spread."*

UNKNOWN

---

THE GOLDEN GATE BRIDGE ROSE OUT OF THE WATER LIKE A COLOSSAL gateway to another world. Its towers pierced through the fog, and the vibrant hue of International Orange gleamed against the muted grays of the sky.

The bridge was an engineering masterpiece that, from a distance, seemed like a floating marvel of engineering and artistry.

But to Mr. John Kevin Hines, it seemed to be the fast path out of misery, out of depression, an escape from earth. John had been struggling with bipolar disease, and episodes of paranoid delusions had forced him to withdraw from college. He stood on the bridge and looked down into the swirling water, poised to jump. Several people walked by him, lost in their own thoughts and agendas, totally unaware that he was about to attempt suicide.

One woman did stop, but only to ask him if he would take a picture. He later recounted that her request, for some reason, added to his sense of loneliness. She walked away. And he jumped.

He is one of just a few people to survive jumping off the Golden Gate Bridge, and he is now a suicide prevention speaker. He has shared with audiences that he believes if even one person had smiled at him, or noticed him, he would not have jumped.

There are countless stories of people on the brink of suicide who changed their minds after a kind word from a stranger. This is the power of positivity. If positivity can save a life, imagine what it can do for yours.

Positive energy is not about denying life's challenges or pasting a smile over heartbreak. It's about making the quiet, deliberate choice to lean into life with hope, to believe in the possibility of a better moment, and to extend that belief to others. It's the stranger who smiles and holds the door for you, reminding you that not all people are bad. It's the random compliment that, even for a moment, allows you to see yourself in a better light.

Here's the thing: a lot of people mistake positive energy as something you either have or you don't. But it isn't magic. It's not reserved for the perpetually cheery or for people who were born optimistic. It is a choice; a practice of choosing to see beyond the immediate difficulty.

For those who find it hard to believe in "positive thinking," this chapter isn't about forcing happiness. It's about cultivating a mindset where positive energy isn't an impossible ideal or an out-of-reach trait, but an ally you can call upon whenever you need it.

Mindfulness and intentionality are essential in cultivating positive energy. When we practice mindfulness, we anchor ourselves in the present moment, appreciating life's simple joys and recognizing the opportunities around us. Intentionality helps us make conscious choices aligned with our values, ensuring that our energy remains focused on what truly matters.

The beauty of positive energy lies in its ability to create a ripple effect. Acts of kindness, expressions of gratitude, and moments of shared joy resonate beyond the individual, touching everyone within reach. This interconnectedness amplifies its impact, creating a collective wave of positivity that influences entire communities.

Positive energy is not limited to fleeting moments of happiness—it is a state of being we can choose. It is a deliberate choice to engage with life in ways that amplify love, joy, fulfillment, and connection. As we tap into this dynamic force, we not only transform our own experiences but also contribute to a more vibrant, interconnected world.

Positive energy lies at the heart of self-worth. Although intangible, it is an undeniable force that breathes life into our experiences. Positive energy is the luminous current that flows from thoughts, emotions, and actions rooted in love, kindness, and joy. It is the gentle vibration that accompanies inspiration, the warmth of genuine connection, and the quiet strength that propels us forward.

The texture of this positive energy is distinct from the old energy narratives that governed the past. It feels more real, grounded, and reflective of our deepest truths. Positive energy resonates with our authentic selves, aligning with what we believe in is the core of our being. It creates a sense of purpose and belonging, grounding us in the knowledge that we are exactly where we need to be on our journey.

Unlike the absence of negativity, positive energy is an active force that shapes our perspectives, decisions, and interactions. It is the undercurrent that makes challenges seem surmountable and possibilities more accessible. When we cultivate positive energy, we unlock the capacity to see life's inherent beauty, even amid adversity. It fosters a mindset of gratitude, resilience, and optimism, creating a fertile ground for growth and joy. One important way to realize if you are stepping into positive energy vs negative energy is to feel the energy of a given challenge. Let us take, for example, a physical challenge such as going to the gym. Are you there to "improve" something, or to "prove" something? If you can identify that your motivation is from within and that you are there to improve yourself and not prove something to someone else, you now have a benchmark for what positive energy feels like vs negative energy.

This isn't about denial or seeing the world through rose-colored glasses. Life is sometimes hard and unfair. It will throw challenges at us left and right. The idea is not to pretend everything is perfect, but rather to choose to believe that there is a plan of a Higher order.

What if the trials you are facing are necessary for you to become the person you want and need to be?

What if, in order to hold massive abundance, love, and joy, you have to first grow and evolve?

The key is to start believing that challenges don't happen *to* you but *for* you.

When negative things happen, we often find ourselves asking, "Why is this happening to me?" Unfortunately, we ask it as more of a complaint than a curiosity. That is the shift. When we can learn to genuinely ask "Why might this be happening to me?" we can start thinking of possible positive reasons for our troubles.

Maybe you were left by a partner because a better one awaits.

Maybe you were taken ill because your body needed a break or your life needed redirection.

Maybe in being delayed by a flat tire, you were saved from getting in an accident a mile down the road.

When nothing is certain, anything is possible, so why not choose to partner with positivity?

The impact of positive energy is far-reaching. On a personal level, it promotes well-being, self-confidence, and a deep sense of purpose. In relationships, it strengthens bonds, encourages empathy, and builds supportive communities. On a broader scale, positive energy becomes a catalyst for societal progress, inspiring cooperation and collective well-being.

# CHAPTER 11

# THE STATE OF EXPANSION

---

*"Success in life could be defined as the continued expansion of happiness and the progressive realization of worthy goals."*

DEEPAK CHOPRA

---

PICTURE A BALLOON, JUST OUT OF THE PACKAGE, CRUMPLED UP AND deflated. It's not broken—it's just waiting. It hasn't yet been used to its potential. With each breath of air, it begins to expand, stretching into its intended shape and function. The more it fills, the lighter it becomes, able to float above the ground that once held it. Expansion doesn't just reveal what the balloon can hold; it reveals how high it can rise.

The same is true for humans.

Survival mode feels constricting, deflating, and rooted in fear, but the emotional state of expansion is the complete opposite—it is open, abundant, and rooted in possibility. When we operate from a place of expansion, we align with the deeper flow of life. We move beyond the limiting beliefs and fears that once kept us trapped in a scarcity mindset, and instead, we step into a mindset where opportunity, growth, and fulfillment are not only possible but inevitable.

If you're currently feeling deflated or exhausted, there is nothing inherently wrong with you. You just haven't yet been put to your greatest use. You just need a little air (and some solid intention), and soon you will be performing the function you were meant to and shifting into lightness.

Expansion is about thriving rather than just surviving. It's about growing into the fullest, most authentic version of ourselves, free from the constraints of fear and societal conditioning. In this state, we are not merely reacting to external circumstances—we are creating our reality through deliberate and empowered choices. It is about believing that life is happening for us and not to us.

When we are in a state of expansion, everything feels different. Emotionally, it is a place of joy, peace, and excitement. There is a deep sense of trust in ourselves and the universe. Fear may still exist, but it no longer drives our decisions; instead, it becomes a signal that we are stepping out of our comfort zone and into growth.

In expansion, our emotions serve as allies rather than barriers. We are in touch with what we feel, and instead of resisting emotions like fear, doubt, or uncertainty, we welcome them as part of the human experience. This allows us to process them in a healthy way and move through them without getting stuck.

We feel empowered and energized by the possibilities that lie ahead, and we approach challenges with a mindset of curiosity instead of dread. There is a sense of lightness, an unburdening of the fear-based patterns that once kept us small.

The state of expansion is intrinsically linked to an abundance mindset. In survival, we operate from a belief that there is not enough time, money, love, and opportunity—but in expansion, we believe that there is more than enough for everyone. This shift in perspective opens us up to receiving, whether it be in the form of material wealth, emotional connection, or personal growth.

When we believe in abundance, we no longer hold ourselves back out of fear of loss. We take inspired action toward our goals without worrying about failure or scarcity. We understand that even setbacks are temporary and part of the larger process of growth and evolution. In this state, we are open to giving and receiving freely, understanding that life operates in cycles and that what we put into the world will return to us in one form or another.

This abundance mindset allows us to experience life as a continuous flow of opportunities. We stop clinging to the few things we have out of fear of losing them and instead trust that new opportunities, experiences, and relationships will continue to come our way.

One of the most profound shifts that occurs when we move into a state of expansion is the feeling of emotional freedom. In survival, we are bound by our fears, our need for control, and our desire to avoid discomfort. But in expansion, we let go of those chains and step into a space where we can feel whatever arises without being ruled by it.

This emotional freedom allows us to navigate life's challenges with grace and resilience. Instead of being paralyzed by fear or overwhelmed by uncertainty, we allow ourselves to feel it, process it, and move forward regardless. We no longer need to micromanage every aspect of our lives to avoid discomfort because we trust in our ability to handle whatever comes our way.

When I was in a state of survival, I seemed to carry a belief that everyone and everything was out to get me. Can you relate?

I took others' comments personally. I felt like a victim. I could not accept criticism in any form. Even a rainy day felt like a personal attack sent by the universe to muck up my plans!

When I learned to shift into expansion, however, I realized that I am an extra in other people's stories. I am one soul in a giant cosmic soup full of people all doing the best they can with what they've got.

Realizing that you are on your own path and that most of what happens during the day is out of your hands is quite freeing. All you need to do is choose whether to either view it through the lens of a resentful victim, or through the lens of a trusting, expansive receiver.

Emotional freedom is also about releasing the need for external validation. When we are in a state of expansion, we are no longer driven by the need to prove ourselves to others. We recognize that our worth is inherent, not dependent on the approval or opinions of those around us. This self-assurance allows us to show up authentically, express ourselves freely, and pursue our true passions without fear of judgment or rejection.

A hallmark of the emotional state of expansion is living in a state of flow. Flow is a psychological state in which we are fully immersed in the present moment, deeply focused, and effortlessly moving through life. In flow, time seems to disappear, and everything feels effortless and aligned. This happens because we are not resisting life or trying to control every outcome; instead, we are working in harmony with the energy around us.

When we live in expansion, flow becomes a natural part of our daily experience. We are more in tune with our intuition and follow its guidance without hesitation. We trust that things will unfold as they are meant to, and we are open to the unexpected twists and turns that life may bring.

This state of flow allows us to tap into our creativity, problem-solving abilities, and innovation in ways that are inaccessible in survival mode. It is as if the mental fog clears, and we can see possibilities and solutions that were not visible before. When we are in flow, we are at our most productive, not because we are pushing ourselves harder, but because we are working with the natural rhythm of life rather than against it.

In the emotional state of expansion, we become creators of our reality. We move beyond simply reacting to life and begin actively shaping it. This creative power comes from a place of alignment with our true desires and values. We are no longer creating from a place of fear or lack but from a place of love, purpose, and vision.

Moving into a state of expansion, especially during challenging times, requires intention, courage, and actionable steps. Here's a guide to help you start breathing life into your potential, even when everything feels deflated:

### 1. Start with Small Breaths of Intention

Like the balloon that begins with a single puff of air, expansion doesn't require an immediate leap into greatness. It starts with small, intentional actions. Begin by asking yourself:

- What is one thing I can do today that feels nourishing or uplifting?
- What small action can I take that aligns with my values or desires?

Even tiny steps—such as journaling for five minutes, going for a walk, or reaching out to a friend—can create a ripple effect of momentum.

### 2. Shift Your Perspective

When life feels constricting, it's often because our focus is narrowed on what's not working or what we lack. To break free from this mindset:

- **Practice gratitude:** Each day, write down three things you're grateful for, no matter how small. Gratitude shifts your focus from scarcity to abundance.

- **Ask empowering questions:** Instead of asking, "Why is this happening to me?" ask, "What can this teach me?" or "How can I grow from this?" or my favorite, "Does this really have anything to do with me or is it just happening AROUND me?"

3. **Connect with Your Vision**

When life feels heavy, reconnecting with your purpose and vision can reignite your inner flame. To do this:

- **Visualize your expanded self:** Close your eyes and picture yourself thriving. How do you feel? What does your life look like? Use this vision as a compass.
- **Create a "why" statement:** Write down why you want to grow or expand. Let this "why" fuel you on difficult days.
- Do something, anything, that inspires you without dismissing it as a waste of time. Paint, exercise, write, travel, volunteer. Put yourself to good use and eventually, your purpose will reveal itself.

4. **Anchor Yourself in the Present**

Expansion thrives in the present moment, not in dwelling on the past or worrying about the future. Ground yourself by:

- **Practicing mindfulness:** Focus on your breath or engage fully in a simple activity like sipping tea or walking.
- **Using affirmations:** Repeat phrases like "I am exactly where I need to be" or "I trust the process of life."

### 5. Cultivate an Abundance Mindset

Expansion flourishes when you believe there is enough for you and others. To shift from scarcity to abundance:

- **Celebrate others' successes:** Use them as evidence that success is possible for you, too.
- **Give freely:** Whether it's your time, a kind word, or resources, giving opens the door for receiving.

### 6. Trust the Flow of Life

Expansion isn't about forcing outcomes; it's about aligning with life's natural rhythms. To step into flow:

- **Surrender control:** Let go of the need to micromanage every detail. Trust that things will unfold in their own time.
- **Follow your intuition:** Pay attention to the quiet nudges and instincts guiding you toward what feels right.

When you feel deflated, remind yourself of the balloon. It was never broken—only waiting for the breath of life to reveal its potential. You, too, are not broken. Your expansion is not only possible, but inevitable. Begin with one breath, one small act of courage, and soon, you will find yourself rising above the ground that once held you. Ultimately, we can only be responsible for our own thoughts, feelings, and actions, not those of others.

# CHAPTER 12
# EMBRACING THE UNKNOWN

---

*"Let go of certainty. The opposite isn't uncertainty. It's openness, curiosity and a willingness to embrace paradox, rather than choose up sides. The ultimate challenge is to accept ourselves exactly as we are, but never stop trying to learn and grow."*

TONY SCHWARTZ

---

I LOVE THAT QUOTE, BUT I WOULD LIKE TO ADD TO IT. THE ULTIMATE challenge is not just to accept ourselves exactly as we are, but to accept the moment exactly as it is.

Humans are masters of self-inflicted pain. We replay imagined disasters in our minds, agonize over scenarios that may never come to pass, and cling to the illusion of control like a lifeline in a storm. In our refusal to embrace the unknown, we tie ourselves to never-ending fear. The need for certainty can trap us in an endless cycle of anxiety, where every twist and turn in life feels like a threat rather than an opportunity. Our natural tendency to avoid threats then paralyzes us into complete inaction.

Have you seen the movie *Finding Nemo*?? In it, a father fish is so protective of his son that he refuses to let him try anything new, go anywhere unfamiliar, or have any adventures at all. He says, "I promised I would never let anything happen to him."

His wise friend Dory says, "Well, that's a funny thing to promise. You can't never let anything happen to him. Then nothing would ever happen to him."

Think about that. If we protect ourselves from the unknown under the assumption that the unknown is bad, we are also protecting ourselves from the possibility that the unknown is extraordinary.

Breaking free from the familiar narrative and stepping into the unknown is not easy. It requires us to confront our fears, let go of old beliefs, and trust in the power of our own energy to guide us. But the rewards of this journey are immense.

By embracing the unknown, we open ourselves up to new possibilities and new forms of wealth—wealth that goes beyond money and status to include love, connection, purpose, and meaning. This is the path to true fulfillment, and it is available to all of us if we are willing to take the first step.

To embrace the unknown is to understand that life is not a fixed path, and it is not meant to be fully mapped out. The unknown is where all creation and innovation spring from—it is where the potential for new ideas, new experiences, and new realities are born. When we embrace the unknown, we tap into a reservoir of possibilities beyond anything we can imagine, unlocking the potential for limitless growth.

Consider how every great invention, breakthrough, or personal transformation in history has come from stepping into the unknown. Whether it's launching a business, pursuing a passion, or moving to a new city, all significant progress happens when we venture beyond what we already know.

By embracing the unknown, we learn to trust ourselves and our intuition more deeply. We develop resilience, creativity, and problem-solving skills that would have otherwise remained dormant. We discover inner strengths we did not know we had and cultivate a sense of self-confidence that is rooted in our ability to navigate uncertainty rather than control outcomes.

Unfortunately, we live in a world that prizes certainty and predictability. We are taught to plan, to know, and to control as much as possible to feel safe. Yet, in the heart of the unknown lies the secret to the most profound growth, discovery, and transformation. Embracing the unknown is not only about stepping into the future without fear but also about acknowledging that true magic happens when we let go of the need to know everything and open ourselves up to the infinite possibilities life has to offer.

The first step toward embracing the unknown is to reframe it. Instead of seeing the unknown as a threat, we can choose to view it as a space of endless possibility. The unknown is not something to fear; it is a blank canvas where we can paint whatever future we desire.

When we embrace the unknown, we step out of the narrow constraints of what we think is possible and open ourselves up to limitless potential. We allow ourselves to dream bigger, take bolder actions, and invite new opportunities into our lives that we could not have predicted or planned for.

We also become more open to learning. We release the need to be "right" or to have all the answers, and instead, approach life with curiosity and a willingness to grow. This shift in perspective allows us to see every new challenge as an opportunity for expansion rather than a threat.

Embracing the unknown requires a deep sense of trust—both in ourselves and in the universe. It is about surrendering to the flow of life and recognizing that we do not need to have everything figured out in order to move forward. In fact, trying to control every outcome often limits us, because we are operating from the narrow confines of what we already know.

When we surrender to the flow, we allow life to unfold in ways that are beyond our current understanding. We trust that the universe has a greater plan for us, one that we may not be able to see in the moment but that is leading us toward our highest good. This surrender is not passive; it is an active choice to let go of control and trust in the process.

Surrendering to the unknown also means being open to the possibility that what we desire may manifest in ways we did not expect. Often, when we set out on a new path, the universe delivers opportunities that are even better than what we had envisioned. But these opportunities can only come if we are willing to let go of rigid expectations and allow life to surprise us.

Living in this state of openness is incredibly empowering. It means that we are no longer bound by the need for approval or the fear of making mistakes. We are free to take risks, to follow our intuition, and to pursue what lights us up, even if we do not know exactly where it will lead. This freedom allows us to live more authentically, aligning our actions with our true desires rather than playing it safe in order to meet others' expectations.

Stepping into the unknown takes courage. It is important to remember that courage is not the absence of fear—it is the willingness to move forward in the presence of fear.

Every time we choose to embrace the unknown, we strengthen our courage muscle. We begin to trust ourselves more, knowing that no matter what happens, we have the capacity to navigate whatever comes our way. This courage builds momentum, and the more we practice stepping into the unknown, the more comfortable we become with uncertainty.

It is also important to remember that we do not have to make giant leaps into the unknown all at once. We can start small, taking one step at a time into unfamiliar territory, testing the waters, and building our confidence as we go. Every small act of courage accumulates, and over time, it leads to profound transformation.

When we approach life with the belief that the unknown is where our greatest potential lies, we begin to welcome uncertainty rather than resist it.

This mindset allows us to navigate change with grace and adaptability. It helps us remain flexible in the face of challenges and open to new opportunities, even when they come disguised as setbacks. In this way, the unknown becomes our ally, not our enemy. It becomes the space where we discover who we truly are and what we are capable of. It becomes the birthplace of our dreams, our breakthroughs, and our greatest achievements.

Embracing the unknown is the key to unlocking our limitless potential. It is where the magic of life resides—the space where we can create, grow, and evolve in ways we never imagined. By stepping into the unknown with courage and trust, we open ourselves up to a life of possibility, where anything is possible, and everything is an opportunity for expansion.

In the unknown, we discover that we are far more powerful than we ever realized and that life offers more abundance than we could have ever imagined. In this discovery process, we unlock the true essence of who we are—limitless, expansive, and capable of creating a life beyond our wildest dreams.

When we finally release our grip on control and step into the unknown, everything changes. The moment we surrender to life's unpredictability, we open the door to possibility. Letting go is not an act of giving up—it's an act of courage, a declaration of trust in something greater than our limited perspective. In this space of surrender, we find freedom. Our energy shifts from bracing for the worst to embracing what is. Life begins to flow naturally like an unblocked river finally flowing freely. We become more present, more at peace, and more attuned to the beauty that exists in the here and now. It is in this letting go that we rediscover the joy we had been chasing all along, only to find it was waiting within us the entire time.

# CHAPTER 13
# NAVIGATING CHALLENGES WITH INTEGRITY

---

*"Challenges are what make life interesting. Overcoming them is what makes life meaningful."*

JOSH MARINE

---

ON JANUARY 15, 2009, US AIRWAYS FLIGHT 1549 HAD JUST TAKEN OFF when a flock of geese struck the aircraft, causing the catastrophic failure of both engines. The situation was dire. Airline captain Chesley "Sully" Sullenberger and his crew had less than four minutes to decide how to save the lives of the 155 people on board.

Many pilots in this situation might have panicked or taken the route of attempting to return to LaGuardia Airport.

However, Sully's integrity as a leader and his commitment to the safety of his passengers guided his actions. He meticulously assessed the situation, communicated clearly with air traffic control, and determined that the best chance for survival was to land the plane on the Hudson River. It was a decision that defied convention and carried enormous risk, but it was made with calm precision and unwavering adherence to his duty.

The outcome of his choice was nothing short of miraculous. Sullenberger successfully landed the plane on the icy waters of the Hudson, and all 155 people aboard survived. The event, later dubbed the "Miracle on the Hudson," was a testament to the power of integrity and the courage to act decisively in alignment with core values.

Integrity is not the absence of challenges but the refusal to compromise our values when those challenges arise. It is in the midst of adversity that our character is truly tested and profoundly shaped. To navigate obstacles with integrity is to align our actions with our principles, even when it's inconvenient, unpopular, risky, or costly.

Upholding your values when the going gets tough requires courage, resilience, and the ability to embrace discomfort. But it is through these challenges that you grow. By navigating obstacles with integrity, you build a stronger character and gain the respect of those around you—and, most importantly, of yourself.

The way we respond to these challenges defines not only the outcome of the situation but also the trajectory of our lives. At the heart of successfully navigating difficult moments lies one essential quality: integrity.

Sullenberger's story reminds us that challenges will always come, often in unexpected forms. But when we respond with integrity, keeping our eyes on the target of our purpose and our primary goal, we not only solve the immediate problem, we also inspire trust, respect, and admiration from those around us. Navigating challenges with integrity transforms adversity into an opportunity for growth and impact, leaving a legacy far greater than any fleeting success.

Integrity is more than just honesty; it is the practice of staying true to your principles and authentic self, especially in the face of seemingly insurmountable challenges. It is about standing firm in your truth and making choices that reflect who you are at your core. When we face challenges with integrity, we can navigate them with grace, resilience, and purpose, ensuring that the decisions we make, no matter how difficult, align with our highest selves.

To navigate challenges with integrity means to approach difficult situations from a place of alignment with your values and truth, rather than reacting out of fear, pressure, or the need for immediate gratification. Integrity acts as an internal compass, guiding us to make decisions that reflect our highest principles, even when taking the easy way out might seem tempting. What seems like an uncomplicated way may reveal itself to be the most difficult way over time.

It is natural to feel vulnerable or uncertain in the face of challenges, but integrity asks us to step back and consider the bigger picture. It asks us to think about how our actions in these moments will impact our sense of self, others, and our long-term goals. When we act from a place of integrity, we make decisions that are not just beneficial in the short term but that resonate with our true values and ensure sustainable success.

Furthermore, challenges reveal whether we are truly committed to living by our principles or if we will abandon them when the road becomes difficult. In difficult situations, it can be easy to justify actions that go against our values, particularly if they seem to offer a quick fix.

In 1995, a fire destroyed the textile factory of Aaron Feuerstein, owner of Malden Mills, putting the livelihoods of 3,000 employees at risk. Faced with immense pressure to relocate operations to a cheaper location, Aaron chose instead to rebuild the factory in the same community and continued to pay his workers during the reconstruction period.

Many questioned his decision, as it was far more costly than taking the path of least resistance.

Yet, Aaron's deep commitment to his employees and the values of loyalty and compassion guided him. He believed that taking the business out of the community and abandoning his workers, many of whom had been with the company for years, would betray his principles and undermine the trust he had built.

Though the decision placed financial strain on the company, it earned Aaron widespread respect and loyalty. His actions demonstrated that integrity could take precedence over profit. While the business eventually faced challenges in the competitive marketplace, Aaron's commitment to doing the right thing left a lasting legacy, inspiring countless others in the business world to prioritize people over profits.

We might not always know the immediate solution to a problem, but acting with integrity ensures that we remain grounded and focused on what truly matters. It creates a sense of inner peace, knowing that we stayed true to our values, even when it was difficult.

We must first realize that all challenges are perceived challenges. It is always subjective. What may be a challenge for one person may be easily dealt with or even go unnoticed by someone else. We can categorize these challenges into difficult challenges and challenges of choice.

Difficult challenges feel insurmountable. They cause us anxiety, frustration, and stress, and have a negative energy attached to them. Challenges of choice, however, are those challenges we welcome into our lives to give us a sense of learning, growth, and accomplishment. We see them positively and look forward to engaging them. We can choose how we view our challenges. We are under no obligation in this life to only view our challenges as difficult struggles that we can barely survive. We can accept and create challenges that we see as gifts of knowledge, growth, and experience. In business and life, I considered one of my superpowers to be that I could hold the hot coal the longest. That is, I would create and take on challenges that were so very difficult that others would not want to take them on or not be able to outlast me, and I knew I could persist longer than the challenge.

We can choose to accept challenges that are delivered with grace and joy through a beautiful path. When we recognize the energy and motive behind the challenge we are creating, we start to evolve our challenges and are able to choose challenges that originate from a state of improving something and not proving something.

One of the most difficult aspects of maintaining integrity during challenges is the uncertainty that often accompanies these moments. When we do not know how a situation will unfold or what the outcome will be, it can be tempting to abandon our principles in favor of what is perceived as security or control. However, it is precisely during these uncertain times that integrity is most important.

Integrity is not about knowing all the answers; it is about trusting in the strength of your convictions, even when the path ahead is unclear. This requires courage and a willingness to embrace discomfort. When we cultivate integrity, we learn to stay rooted in our truth, even when external circumstances are chaotic or unpredictable.

While integrity is about staying true to your principles, it is important to recognize that there is a difference between integrity and rigidity. Navigating challenges with integrity does not mean being inflexible or refusing to adapt when circumstances change. Rather, it is about finding a balance between staying grounded in your core values while remaining open to new possibilities and solutions.

In challenging situations, flexibility allows us to explore different perspectives and approaches, while integrity ensures that we do not lose sight of our authentic selves in the process. For example, if you are facing a personal or professional conflict, integrity might mean holding firm to your values of honesty and respect, while flexibility allows you to find creative solutions that benefit all parties involved.

For example, in one business negotiation I was a part of, I was purchasing a business from an individual who told me, "If you change anything, you are a damn fool."

His words were particularly challenging because one reason I was considering the business was that I realized the potential changes I could make that, in my mind, would improve it greatly. I contemplated compromising my intentions, and, since I wanted this individual to continue to work in the company, their happiness was also important to me. I sat with this decision for a while to consider how each challenge would feel. Compromising my intention would be a challenge that would potentially last until this individual was no longer associated with the company. Compromising his wishes would affect the culture and function of the company in other negative ways. I chose to sit down with them and explain all of the potential challenges that I was facing and ask them what challenges they had been dealing with as well. It turned out that we were both much more aligned than either of us realized. We were able to let go of the preconceived difficult challenges that we could both only see separately before, and construct new challenges that would allow both of us to stay true to our authenticity and intentions, as well as make effective and impactful changes to move the business forward.

This balance is essential for growth. When we approach challenges with both integrity and flexibility, we create opportunities for learning and transformation, rather than becoming stuck in fixed ways of thinking or behaving.

In relationships, integrity fosters trust, respect, and open communication, as well as allowing for personal boundaries and self-care. When we consistently act in alignment with our values, others know that they can depend on us to be honest, fair, and considerate, even during times of conflict or challenge. This strengthens the bond we share with those around us and creates an environment where respect, mutual support, and understanding can flourish.

In a world that often values quick fixes and external success, choosing to live with integrity may not always be the easiest path, but it is undoubtedly the most rewarding. It ensures that no matter what challenges come our way, we can move through them with a sense of peace, knowing that we have acted in alignment with our highest selves.

And the universe rewards us for doing so. Karma is not just a buzz-word; it's a frequency. The rewards may not come immediately... but they will come.

# CHAPTER 14
# CULTIVATING SELF-AWARENESS

---

*"Your vision will become clear only when you can look into your own heart. Who looks outside, dreams; who looks inside, awakes."*

CARL JUNG

---

SELF-AWARENESS ACTS AS A BEACON, ILLUMINATING THE PATH TO alignment.

The challenge? It isn't pretty. Often, when we commit to self-awareness, we are committing to holding up a mirror that reflects back to us the most wounded part of ourselves. It is not for the faint of heart, but a practice of self-awareness not only keeps you aligned with your right path, it protects you from creating unnecessary drama in your life.

First, regularly check in with yourself and ask: *Are my actions and decisions aligned with my core values?* This practice of reflection deepens your connection to your integrity. It allows you to adjust and realign when necessary, keeping you on the right path and ensuring your actions remain true to your beliefs.

We've got to make regular practice out of looking inward, understanding our thoughts, emotions, actions, and motivations, and seeing ourselves clearly in relation to the world around us.

Without self-awareness, we are like passengers in a vehicle with no control over where we are headed. With self-awareness, however, we become the drivers of our own lives, able to make conscious choices that reflect who we truly are and what we want to achieve. It allows us to recognize when we are acting out of habit, fear, or societal expectations rather than from our true desires and values.

Without self-awareness, it is easy to fall into autopilot mode—reacting to situations, making decisions based on external pressures, and getting caught in patterns that do not serve us. We may find ourselves stuck in jobs, relationships, or lifestyles that do not align with our true selves, simply because we have not taken the time to reflect on what truly matters to us.

Second, recognize that self-awareness is the warrior's discipline of catching ourselves, swiftly and without apology, in the act of creating our own suffering. It requires noticing when we're spinning tall tales, distorting reality, or reacting to the present moment from our past wounds and programming. It is the quiet practice of pausing, checking in with the truth, and choosing mastery over sabotage.

Imagine you've just sent a message to a friend, and they haven't replied for hours. Almost instantly, your mind might start spinning:

*They're upset. I must have said something wrong. Maybe they're pulling away.*

The story snowballs, and before you know it, you're anxious and questioning the entire friendship. If you let it get out of hand, you may shoot off a second nasty text to that friend demanding to know why they are ignoring you. Meanwhile, if you knew the truth, you would know that they are in a meeting and their phone is turned off. They haven't even seen the message from you.

This is where self-awareness steps in. If you're paying close attention, you'll catch yourself the moment the story begins—the shift from reality (no reply yet) to your assumption (something is wrong).

You recognize that this emotional spiral isn't the truth; it's a narrative you created. With self-awareness, you pause and ask: *Is this real, or am I creating a false story?* Then, with self-mastery, you choose not to engage in the story and redirect your focus, saving yourself from unnecessary suffering and drama. Moments like these are where growth happens. Recognizing the pattern fast is the key to keeping your peace.

One of the best ways to embody self-awareness is to cultivate a practice of regular reflection. Reflection is the practice of taking time to examine your thoughts, emotions, behaviors, and experiences.

Reflection is essential to self-awareness because it creates the space needed for introspection. In the midst of daily life, we are often too focused on external events, responsibilities, and distractions to pay attention to what is happening inside of us. This practice allows us the opportunity to pause, step back, and examine our inner landscape with fresh eyes. When we move forward from a point of reflection instead of reaction, we will find that regardless of the outcome, we have deeper confidence in our decisions and can not only expect a better result but also be better equipped to manage results that do not align with our expectations.

This practice can take many forms, from journaling and meditation to simply sitting quietly and contemplating our experiences. Whatever form it takes, the goal of reflection is to deepen our understanding of ourselves so that we can make more conscious choices in our lives.

The process of reflecting regularly on our experiences and emotions has numerous benefits for our overall well-being and personal development. Some of the key benefits include:

1. **Clarity and Focus:** When we take the time to reflect on our thoughts and actions, we gain clarity about what is truly important to us. We become more aware of our priorities, values, and goals, which allows us to focus our energy on what matters most.

2. **Emotional Intelligence:** Reflection helps us to better understand our emotions, as well as the triggers and underlying beliefs that shape them. As we become more aware of our emotional patterns, we can respond to situations with greater emotional intelligence, rather than reacting impulsively.

3. **Improved Decision-Making:** Self-awareness enables us to make decisions that are aligned with our authentic selves. By reflecting on past decisions, we can learn from our experiences and make more intentional choices in the future.

4. **Personal Growth:** Through reflection, we can identify areas where we want to grow and develop. Whether it is cultivating new skills, changing habits, or improving relationships, self-awareness allows us to recognize the steps we need to take to become the best version of ourselves.

5. **Resilience:** When we are aware of our internal landscape, we are better equipped to navigate challenges and setbacks. Reflection helps us to process difficult emotions, learn from adversity, and approach challenges with a growth mindset.

There are many different methods for practicing reflection, and the key is to find the approach that resonates most with you. Here are a few effective methods for cultivating self-awareness through reflection:

1. **Journaling:** Writing down your thoughts, feelings, and experiences in a journal is one of the most powerful tools for self-reflection. Journaling allows you to process your emotions, gain insights into your patterns, and track your growth over time. To get started, set aside a few minutes each day to write about your experiences, thoughts, and how you are feeling. Over time, you will begin to notice recurring themes and gain a deeper understanding of your inner world.

2. **Meditation:** Meditation is another excellent practice for cultivating self-awareness. By sitting quietly and focusing on your breath, you create space to observe your thoughts and emotions without judgment. Meditation helps you to become more aware of your mental and emotional patterns, as well as develop a sense of inner calm and clarity.

3. **Mindful Reflection:** Mindful reflection involves taking a few moments throughout your day to pause and check in with yourself. Ask yourself questions like, "How am I feeling emotionally right now?", "How is this making me feel physically?" or "What thoughts are running through my mind?" This simple practice helps you to stay connected with your inner self, even in the midst of daily activities.

4. **Reflective Questions:** Asking yourself reflective questions is a great way to gain deeper insights into your behavior and motivations. Some powerful questions to ask include:
   - "What are my authentic values, and how am I living in alignment with them?"
   - "What fears or limiting beliefs are holding me back?"
   - "What patterns do I notice in my relationships, work, or personal life?"
   - "What lessons have I learned from recent experiences, and how can I apply them going forward?"

○ What could I have done differently?

5. **Engaging in Conversations:** Sometimes, self-awareness comes from engaging in deep conversations with others. Talking about your thoughts and experiences with a trusted friend, mentor, or coach can help you gain new perspectives and insights into yourself. Others can often reflect back to us things we might not see on our own, offering valuable feedback for growth.

Self-awareness is cultivated through touchstones that guide us in understanding who we truly are, what we value, and what we genuinely want and need. These touchstones are not rigid rules but a living framework that helps us build the foundation for the reality we create.

Compassion is one such cornerstone, a gentle yet powerful practice of doing no harm. Everyone has a story, and meeting others with compassion frees us from the weight of judgment and negativity. It softens the edges of how we are seen in return.

Moderation is another grounding force that asks us to define what is truly enough. It pulls us out of the endless pursuit of more and into the calm clarity of knowing when we have what we need. This clarity frees us from the illusion of lack, fostering confidence in our ability to live without constant seeking. Integrity, too, is essential—a steady compass that keeps us aligned with our deepest values.

Flow reminds us that life is not fixed, that attention and energy are in constant motion. The sensations of ease and discomfort are guides, telling us when we are in alignment and when we've veered off course. Discomfort is not a warning to retreat, but a signal to pause, reflect, and ask: What is this trying to show me? Change is not the enemy—it is life's way of inviting us to realign with what matters most.

All of this comes together through focus, the quiet force that sharpens our awareness. Energy flows where attention goes. When we focus on our inner experience without judgment, we unlock the clarity needed for transformation. Everything we observe, we can change. And with clarity, everything begins to shift. Focus allows us to see ourselves clearly, and in that seeing, true self-awareness takes root. From there, we stop merely reacting to life and begin living with purpose, presence, and deep inner freedom.

The key to cultivating self-awareness through reflection is consistency. It is not enough to reflect occasionally; instead, make it a regular practice in your life.

It is also important to approach reflection with an open and non-judgmental mindset. The goal is not to criticize or judge yourself, but to observe and understand. Be curious about what comes up during your reflections and give yourself permission to explore your inner world without self-criticism.

Over time, you will notice the profound impact that reflection has on your life. As your self-awareness deepens, you will gain greater clarity about who you are, what you want, and how you can live in alignment with your true self.

# CHAPTER 15
# EMBRACING ACCOUNTABILITY

---

*"Accountability is the glue that ties commitment to the result."*

BOB PROCTOR

---

ACCOUNTABILITY BRIDGES THE GAP BETWEEN INTENTION AND ACTION and between wishes and reality.

It's the fierce act of owning your choices—every thought, every action, every consequence—without excuse or deflection. In that ownership lies power, because what we refuse to face will quietly control us, but what we confront, we can change.

It requires us, however, to be willing to admit fault. Humans hate that.

How often have you heard someone say something like, "It wasn't my fault" or "That's not my responsibility." Owning our mistakes is uncomfortable because admitting fault threatens the ego's fragile sense of control and forces us to confront the uncomfortable truth that we are imperfect, vulnerable, and sometimes the source of our own suffering.

Yet, it is in accountability that our strength as leaders, both of ourselves and of others, is awakened and honed. When you fall short of your ideals, own it. Taking responsibility for your choices, both good and bad, fosters humility and builds trust. Embracing accountability not only strengthens your integrity but also creates an environment of openness and transparency, both within yourself and in your relationships with others.

Accountability is often seen as a responsibility we owe to others, but in reality, it is a powerful practice that begins with ourselves. Being accountable means taking full ownership of our actions, decisions, and the outcomes that follow. Accountability is not just about admitting mistakes; it is about standing in our power, understanding the consequences of our actions, and taking proactive steps to create the life we desire.

When we practice accountability, we shift from being passive participants in our lives to becoming active creators of our experiences. We stop blaming external circumstances, other people, or luck for our outcomes and instead take responsibility for how we show up in the world. This shift in mindset is empowering because it reminds us that we have the ability to influence our lives and direct our energy toward what truly matters.

At its core, accountability is about recognizing our agency—our ability to make choices and influence outcomes. When we are accountable, we understand that we are not helpless victims of our circumstances but empowered individuals with the capacity to change our lives. This sense of ownership over our choices and actions is what leads to empowerment.

Empowerment comes from the realization that we have the power to create the life we want. If you break apart the word "responsibility", what it actually means is the ability to respond. It is about acknowledging that while we may not have control over everything that happens to us, we do have control over how we respond and what we do next. Accountability bridges the gap between external circumstances and internal power, reminding us that our actions and decisions matter.

When we hold ourselves accountable, we also develop a stronger sense of self-efficacy—the belief in our ability to achieve our goals. This belief is essential for empowerment because it fuels our confidence and determination to take meaningful action. Every time we take responsibility for our actions, we reinforce the idea that we can create positive change in our lives.

1. **Taking Ownership of Your Life**

One of the key aspects of accountability is taking ownership of your life. This means recognizing that you are responsible for your thoughts, feelings, behaviors, and outcomes. Instead of blaming others for what goes wrong or waiting for someone else to fix things, you take control of your own journey. When you take ownership, you empower yourself to create the change you want to see. You stop giving your power away to circumstances or people and instead focus on what you can do to move forward.

2. **When something challenging happens, you can practice taking full responsibility.**

That doesn't mean assuming fault, but rather taking full responsibility for how you will respond to the situation to turn it in the direction of the highest good for all involved. Real Control vs False Control: Real control looks like inaction, feels like surrender, and only involves you. False control looks like action, feels like fear, and always involves someone else. It is important to identify and distinguish what is taking control of your life and what is simply manipulation. The power of true control is that in any circumstance, you have the confidence that you are acting in alignment with your authentic values. You cannot own or control the thoughts, feelings, or actions of others, only your own.

### 3. Acknowledging Your Role in Success and Failure

Accountability requires you to be honest about both your successes and your failures. It is easy to take credit for your achievements, but true accountability also means acknowledging when you have made mistakes, fallen short, or chosen a path that did not lead to the desired outcome. This kind of honesty is a powerful tool for growth because it allows you to learn from your experiences.

### 4. Setting Clear Goals and Intentions

Accountability is closely tied to goal setting. When you are accountable, you take the time to set clear goals and intentions for yourself, and you commit to following through on them. This practice helps you stay focused on what truly matters to you and ensures that your actions align with your values and desires.

### 5. Facing Challenges with Resilience

Accountability empowers you to face challenges with resilience. When things do not go as planned, accountability helps you avoid falling into a victim mindset. Instead of feeling defeated by obstacles, you take responsibility for how you respond to them. You recognize that challenges are a part of life, and while you cannot control every obstacle, you can control how you navigate them.

---

The good news is that accountability is ideally not a solo journey. Finding an accountability partner can give you the extra layer of support you need to stay consistent. This could be a friend, mentor, or coach; someone who checks in with you, asks the hard questions and helps you stay on track. Sharing your goals and challenges with someone else adds a layer of commitment and gives you fresh perspectives and feedback that you might miss on your own.

Mistakes will inevitably happen, but how you respond is what defines your growth. Acknowledge what went wrong, reflect on the experience, and use it as a chance to learn and adjust.

Just as important as owning your mistakes is celebrating your successes. Accountability is not solely about pointing out where you fall short—it's about recognizing and honoring your progress. Take time to acknowledge the wins, no matter how small. Celebrating these moments reinforces the belief that you are capable, that progress is happening, and that you have what it takes to achieve your goals. Each success, no matter how minor, is proof of your growth and a source of momentum to carry you forward.

Embracing accountability in all areas of your life has numerous benefits, both personally and professionally. Here are just a few of the positive outcomes that result from practicing accountability:

- **Greater Confidence:** Accountability builds confidence by reinforcing the belief that you are in control of your life. Each time you take responsibility for your actions and follow through on your commitments, you prove to yourself that you are capable of achieving your goals.

- **Improved Relationships:** When you practice accountability, you become more reliable and trustworthy. This not only improves your relationship with yourself but also strengthens your relationships with others. People are more likely to respect and trust you when they know you take responsibility for your actions.

- **Increased Productivity:** Accountability helps you stay focused and committed to your goals, which leads to greater productivity. When you hold yourself accountable for taking consistent action, you make steady progress toward your objectives and avoid procrastination.

- **Personal Growth:** Accountability is a powerful tool for personal growth. By consistently reflecting on your actions, learning from your mistakes, and making improvements, you develop greater self-awareness and become more aligned with your authentic self.

- **Empowerment:** Perhaps the most profound benefit of accountability is the sense of empowerment it brings. When you take responsibility for your life, you tap into your inner power and realize that you have the ability to create the reality you desire. Accountability frees you from the limitations of blame and excuses, allowing you to fully embrace your role as the creator of your own destiny.

Your most courageous, aligned, and fulfilling life begins with accountability, and the more you practice it, the more you will realize just how powerful you truly are.

# CHAPTER 16
# THE POWER OF
# EMPOWERMENT

---

*"The most common way that people give up their power is thinking they don't have any."*

ALICE WALKER

---

EMPOWERMENT IS A WORD THAT IS OFTEN USED BUT RARELY FULLY understood.

It is more than just feeling confident or capable—it is about recognizing and activating the deep well of inner strength, agency, and potential that exists within each of us. True empowerment is a state of being in which we take full ownership of our lives, acknowledging that we have the power to shape our circumstances, make decisions aligned with our values, and create the future we desire. It is the opposite of victimhood; it is standing in our own power and using that power to live authentically.

In this chapter, we will explore the transformative nature of empowerment, how it affects every area of life, and how you can cultivate this power within yourself. How do we cultivate it in ourselves when we feel constantly challenged by life?

Empowerment is the process of becoming stronger and more confident in creating your reality. It is about embracing your ability to make decisions, act, and create meaningful change.

It starts with a rebellion against any belief (yours or the beliefs of others) that challenges your agency, ability, and courage. When you are empowered, you no longer wait for someone else to give you permission to live your life—you realize that you are the one who holds the keys to your success, happiness, and fulfillment.

Empowerment is deeply personal. It looks different for everyone because it comes from within, rooted in your unique strengths, values, and desires. What empowers one person may not empower another, but the common thread is that empowerment gives you a sense of agency over your life.

At its core, empowerment is about realizing that you are not at the mercy of your past or external circumstances. While you cannot control everything that happens to you, you can control how you respond, what actions you take, and the mindset you adopt. This recognition is liberating because it shifts your focus from what you cannot do to what you can do, allowing you to direct your energy toward solutions and growth.

## EMPOWERMENT IS A GAME-CHANGER.

When you step into your power, it transforms the way you approach life. Here are some of the ways empowerment can change your life:

I. **Freedom from Limiting Beliefs**

Empowerment allows us to release the limiting beliefs that hold us back from reaching our full potential. The stories we tie to these beliefs might tell us that we are not smart enough, talented enough, or worthy enough to succeed. Empowerment allows you to break free from these mental constraints and accept that you can keep the knowledge of your past without attaching these beliefs to it. Take on the persona of a stubborn child. Think back to a kid on the playground telling you couldn't do something. Most likely your response was, "Oh yeah? Watch me!" Empowerment requires that same kind of stubborn sense of self-belief. When you recognize your power, you understand that your potential is not determined by past experiences, societal expectations, or other people's opinions. You are free to define your own path and make decisions based on what you know to be true about yourself. The you of the future is from this moment forward, not in the past.

### 2. Increased Confidence and Self-Esteem

Empowerment naturally leads to greater confidence and self-esteem. When you take control of your life and make choices that align with your values, you reinforce your belief in yourself. You begin to trust your judgment and feel more capable of handling whatever life throws at you. This confidence is not rooted in arrogance, ego, or the need to prove yourself to others. It comes from a deep inner knowing that you are capable and worthy.

### 3. Resilience in the Face of Challenges

Life is full of challenges, but empowerment equips you to navigate them with resilience. When you feel empowered, you do not crumble under pressure or give up when things get tough. Instead, you face challenges head-on, knowing that you have the inner strength to overcome them. Empowerment gives you the courage to take risks, embrace uncertainty, and keep moving forward even when the path is unclear.

### 4. Aligned Action

Empowerment allows you to take aligned action—action that is in harmony with your values, purpose, and desires. When you are empowered, you are not just reacting to life or going through the motions. Instead, you make intentional choices that reflect who you truly are and what you want to create. This alignment leads to greater fulfillment because your actions are consistent with your authentic self.

### 5. Improved Relationships

Empowerment also improves your relationships. When you are empowered, you no longer rely on others to define your worth or validate your choices. This allows you to engage in healthier, more balanced relationships where mutual respect, trust, and autonomy are present. Empowered individuals do not feel the need to control others or allow themselves to be controlled—they approach relationships from a place of confidence, love, and personal boundaries and responsibility.

### 6. Empowering Others

One of the most beautiful aspects of empowerment is that it is contagious. When you embrace your own power, you naturally inspire and empower those around you. You become a role model for others, showing them that they, too, can take control of their lives and live authentically. Empowerment is a ripple effect—by owning your power, you contribute to a culture of empowerment that lifts others up.

Empowerment does not happen overnight, but it is a practice anyone can cultivate. Here are some steps you can take to embrace your power and become more empowered in your daily life:

### 1. Know Yourself.

The first step to empowerment is self-awareness. You cannot fully step into your power if you do not know who you are and what you stand for. Take time to reflect on your values, strengths, and desires. What truly matters to you? What makes you feel alive? When you have a clear understanding of your authentic values, you are better able to make decisions that align with your truth.

### 2. Take Responsibility for Your Life.

Empowerment is rooted in personal responsibility. To be empowered, you must recognize that you are in control of your life. This means taking responsibility for your choices, actions, and the outcomes they produce. When things do not go as planned, resist the temptation to blame external factors or other people. Instead, ask yourself, "What can I learn from this? How can I move forward in a way that aligns with my authentic values?"

### 3. Set Boundaries.

Empowered individuals set healthy boundaries. They know that they have the right to protect their energy, time, and well-being. Setting boundaries is not about being rigid or unkind—it is about honoring yourself and ensuring that you are not overextending or sacrificing your needs for the sake of others. When you set clear boundaries, you create space for empowerment because you are prioritizing what's profoundly important to you.

### 4. Take action, even when you feel scared.

Empowerment requires action. It is not enough to recognize your power—you must use it. This means taking steps toward your goals, even when it is uncomfortable or uncertain. Empowered people understand that fear is a natural part of growth, but they do not let it stop them. They take risks, knowing that each step they take brings them closer to their desired outcome.

### 5. Trust yourself.

Empowerment is built on self-trust. To feel empowered, you need to trust your intuition, your abilities, and your judgment. This trust comes from experience and from consistently showing up for yourself. When you make decisions that align with your values and follow through on your commitments, you reinforce your belief in yourself. Over time, this self-trust becomes the foundation of your empowerment.

### 6. Surround yourself with supportive people.

While empowerment comes from within, it is important to surround yourself with people who support and uplift you. Seek out relationships that encourage your growth and challenge you to step into your power. Avoid people who drain your energy or try to control your decisions. Empowered individuals thrive in environments where they feel supported and respected.

### 7. Let go of everything that is not yours and does not serve you.

Recognize anything in your life that you are holding onto because you feel you should, rather than because you want it in your life. Releasing whatever you have been holding onto and serving that which does not respond in kind is a powerful way to make space in your life for what you really want.

---

Empowerment is not just a personal journey—it has a ripple effect on the world around you. When individuals are empowered, they contribute to the collective well-being of society.

Empowered people are more likely to take initiative, solve problems, and create positive change in their communities. They are not content to simply follow the status quo—they use their power to challenge injustices, uplift others, and create a better world.

When you embrace your own empowerment, you become a force for good. Your actions inspire others to recognize their power, and together, you contribute to a culture of empowerment that benefits everyone. Empowerment is not about individual success—it is about collective transformation. It is about realizing that we all have the ability to create a world where everyone can thrive.

The power of empowerment is transformative. It liberates you from the constraints of limiting beliefs, external validation, and fear. It allows you to step into your true potential and live a life that is aligned with your deepest values and desires.

Empowerment is not a destination—it is a journey. It requires continuous growth, self-awareness, and intentional action. But the rewards of this journey are profound. When you embrace your power, you not only change your own life but you also inspire and uplift those around you.

Empowerment is your birthright. It is not something you need to earn—it is something you already have within you. All it takes is the courage to recognize it, own it, and use it to create the life you were meant to live.

# CHAPTER 17
# THE LIFE OF AUTHENTICITY:
## VICTORY THROUGH EMPOWERMENT

---

*"To be yourself in a world that is constantly trying to make you something else is the greatest accomplishment."*

RALPH WALDO EMERSON

---

EMPOWERMENT IS THE ULTIMATE EXPRESSION OF PERSONAL FREEDOM.

It is the understanding that you are not a passive participant in life, subject to the whims of fate, but an active creator of your reality and experiences. Living an empowered life means embracing your inherent power and potential, and it creates a profound shift in how you perceive and experience the world around you. There are incredible emotional, mental, and spiritual benefits that come with living a life of empowerment, and it feels so liberating.

Choosing to live an empowered life isn't just a decision—it's a catalyst for positive change that ripples through every aspect of your existence. That one bold choice to live on your own terms creates a ripple of good that extends far beyond what you could ever imagine.

One of the most exhilarating feelings that comes with empowerment is the realization that your potential is limitless. When you embrace empowerment, you recognize that the only real limits are the ones you place on yourself. The boundaries that once seemed rigid or impossible to break through begin to dissolve, and you start to see life as an open field of opportunity.

This sense of possibility brings a natural excitement to your life. Instead of feeling constrained by fear or self-doubt, you become curious and open to new experiences. You approach challenges with a mindset of growth, knowing that every step forward—even the difficult ones—brings you closer to realizing your potential. The world no longer feels small or intimidating; it feels like a vast landscape of opportunities just waiting for you to explore.

You are no longer trying to fit into a mold or live up to someone else's expectations. Instead, you are able to be unapologetically yourself, embracing your quirks, your passions, and your values.

There is an incredible joy in knowing that you are free to be exactly who you are, without needing to hide or alter yourself to fit in. Every choice you make, from the relationships you nurture to the career path you follow, reflects your true self, which creates a profound sense of alignment and fulfillment. When you live authentically, life feels more vibrant and meaningful because every action resonates with your core values.

This joy creates emotional freedom. You are finally able to stop relying on external validation to feel worthy or successful because you understand that your value is inherent and not dependent on the approval of others.

With that shift, you are no longer weighed down by insecurities or the fear of judgment. Instead, you cultivate a deep sense of self-worth that is unshakeable. This emotional freedom allows you to approach life with a calm and steady heart, no longer reacting to every challenge or obstacle with anxiety or stress.

With this emotional freedom comes a profound inner peace. When you are empowered, you are no longer fighting against yourself or struggling to prove your worth. You are in harmony with your own desires, and this creates a deep well of tranquility that carries you through even the most chaotic of situations.

This peace then brings a level of confidence that is both grounding and energizing. You no longer second-guess your decisions or question your ability to succeed. Instead, you trust yourself to navigate the complexities of life with grace and wisdom.

This confidence extends to every aspect of your life. Whether you are making a major career decision, navigating a personal challenge, or exploring a new opportunity, you approach it with the belief that you can make the right choice. This self-assurance allows you to move through life with ease and certainty, knowing that you have the power to shape your reality.

The incredible feeling of being confident in your decisions is one of empowerment's greatest gifts. It eliminates the paralyzing fear of making the wrong choice and replaces it with a calm knowing that no matter what happens, you can handle it.

Empowerment gives you the gift of living with purpose. Instead of drifting through life aimlessly, you have a clear sense of direction and motivation. You know what you stand for, what you want to achieve, and how to get there.

Living with purpose is an incredibly uplifting experience. Every day becomes an opportunity to move closer to your goals and contribute to something greater than yourself. You wake up with a sense of excitement about the work you're doing and the impact you're making, which fills your life with meaning and satisfaction.

This sense of purpose fuels your passion and enthusiasm, allowing you to tackle challenges with resilience and determination. When you are living with purpose, even the difficult moments feel worthwhile because they are part of a larger vision that you are dedicated to bringing to life.

Empowered individuals naturally attract healthier relationships. Because you are grounded in your own self-worth, you are more likely to set and maintain clear boundaries that protect your emotional and mental well-being. This leads to deeper connections where both parties feel supported, valued, and free to be themselves.

Living a life of empowerment also means you have more to give to others. When you are filled with confidence, purpose, and inner peace, you are better able to show up for the people in your life with love, compassion, and strength. Your relationships become a source of joy, growth, and mutual empowerment.

Empowerment brings with it an inner strength that makes you resilient in the face of adversity. Instead of feeling overwhelmed or defeated by challenges, you are able to approach them with a sense of confidence and optimism.

This resilience allows you to face difficulties head-on, without losing your sense of self or direction. You understand that challenges are a natural part of life and that you have the power to overcome them. This belief in your own strength creates a feeling of invincibility, allowing you to weather any storm with grace and determination.

Empowerment does not mean that life becomes easy or free of obstacles. Instead, it means that you have developed the inner resources to handle whatever comes your way.

Ultimately, the most amazing feeling that comes with living a life of empowerment is the realization that you are the artist of your own life, with the ability to shape your reality in any way you choose.

Empowerment is not just a state of being—it is a way of life, one that opens the door to your highest potential and allows you to experience the incredible beauty of living authentically, confidently, and fully alive.

How will you choose to paint the masterpiece of your life? How will you write your own story and play the main character you've always been meant to play? It all starts from within. Nobody knows how to be the best version of you better than you.

Empowerment is not just about what you achieve; it's about who you decide to become. It's about embracing the unwavering truth that you are the architect of your destiny. It's about owning your voice, trusting your instincts, and walking boldly in the direction of your dreams with a deep sense of purpose.

The world is longing for the fullest, most powerful version of you. Will you rise to the challenge? Will you step forward with courage, purpose, and conviction? Will you release the shackles of the past and claim the life that is already yours to create?

Once you begin—once you commit to living with authenticity, passion, and intention—there is no limit to what you can accomplish. The canvas is blank, the stage is set, and the pen is in your hand.

# ACKNOWLEDGMENTS

I would like to start off by saying that there truly are no words for the gratitude I feel toward those that have shaped my journey. I feel so honored that our paths have crossed to enrich each other in deep, meaningful ways.

To my parents, I am so very blessed to have had the parents I did. I did not always believe that I had the parents that I wanted. I can see now how I had exactly the parents I needed. Without your perfect part in my journey I would not be able to see that everyone is human. Everyone is fighting their own demons. Everyone is just out here trying to do the best they can with the tools they have at the time. Without you, I would not be the man that I am today. I love that man, and I love you.

To my current mentors and team. You have shown me unwavering support and encouragement along the way. You have believed in me when my own belief was shaky. To Sierra Melcher and the team at Red Thread Publishing as well as the many authors under it's banner that have always been there for inspiration, thank you. To the AMAZING Lisa Nichols and her team, you have shown me how to see the world with different eyes and connect my head to my heart. I will always now hear my soul speak. To the legendary Jack Canfield, you have lead by example and shown me that if I put purpose and service first, everything else falls into place. To Nick Nanton and his amazing crew at Celebrity Branding Agency, including and not limited to, Ryan Ruff and Jason Thomas for always being my encouragement and creating safety in a new world, Mike Dunn and Carlo for making me look better than I ever thought possible, and Gina Hussar for making my thoughts feelings and words come to life. I could not have done this without you.

To all the mentors, colleagues, partners and friends that have shaped me as I have traveled this beautiful life. Thank you. I remember every moment and hold them close to my heart.

# ABOUT THE AUTHOR

Photo by @MIKEDUNNUSA
for Celebrity Branding
Agency

Dr. Stacey Kevin Frick is a seasoned leader and visionary dedicated to fostering health, well-being, and financial empowerment. After practicing medicine for over 20 years as a veterinarian and serving as CEO of multiple successful businesses, Dr. Frick now dedicates his life to empowering others to lead a life of fulfilling service. His mission is to guide individuals toward lives filled with joy, abundance, and purpose, grounded in authenticity and personal empowerment.

As a sought after author, speaker, teacher and founder of The Empowerment Revolution Dr. Frick merges his extensive leadership expertise and business acumen with holistic well-being practices to create transformative pathways for success. A highly sought-after life coach, author, speaker, and entrepreneur, he specializes in boosting self-confidence, enhancing emotional intelligence, and fostering personal growth. His passion for helping individuals overcome personal and professional barriers defines his career and legacy.

Dr. Frick's journey reflects a multifaceted soul with a deep commitment to knowledge, leadership, and innovation. Beyond his professional accomplishments, he finds inspiration in literature, the arts, and fitness, continually enriching his understanding of the world. His dedication to mental health, holistic healing, alternative medicine, and nutrition demonstrates his unwavering belief in the power of a balanced and health-focused lifestyle.

Through his work, Dr. Frick provides a beacon of inspiration and guidance for those seeking financial abundance, holistic well-being, and a deeper connection to their authentic selves. His leadership exemplifies the transformative power of service, offering tools and motivation to those ready to embark on a journey of growth and self-discovery.

Whether you aspire to professional success, improved health, or a more meaningful life, Dr. Stacey Kevin Frick stands as a trusted guide and mentor. His life's mission is to inspire others, helping them unlock their full potential and embrace a future filled with purpose and fulfillment.

instagram.com/staceykevinfrick

facebook.com/stacey.k.frick

linkedin.com/in/dr-stacey-kevin-frick-8b13614

amazon.com/author/drstaceykevinfrick

# READY TO START YOUR OWN EMPOWERMENT REVOLUTION?

If something you read in this book stirred something in you—it's not a coincidence. It's a call. A reminder that your growth, your power, and your dreams are within reach.

## THIS IS YOUR MOMENT TO STEP INTO THE LIFE YOU DESERVE.

Whether you're looking to bring a powerful keynote to your next event, connect for an interview, or simply want to stay inspired and supported—**I invite you to join our community and be part of The Empowerment Revolution.**

Visit **www.DrStaceyKevinFrick.com** to:

- **Book Dr. Stacey** for conferences, keynotes, or workshops
- **Access free resources** and exclusive content
- **Join the movement** and connect with a powerful, heart-centered community

## YOU WERE NEVER MEANT TO DO THIS ALONE. LET'S RISE TOGETHER.

# ALSO BY DR. STACEY KEVIN FRICK

## Unstoppable: Stories of Grit, Determination, and Perseverance

In this empowering collection led by Lisa Nichols, Dr. Stacey Kevin Frick joins a dynamic group of coauthors to share real-life stories of resilience, courage, and triumph. From rock-bottom moments to breakthrough victories, these stories remind us that perseverance pays off—and that you are stronger than you think.

## MENtal Health: Take It "Like a Man"

In this powerful anthology, Dr. Stacey Kevin Frick joins a courageous group of authors and advocates to challenge outdated ideas of masculinity. *MENtal Health* redefines what it means to "take it like a man" by sharing real, vulnerable stories of mental health struggles—and the strength it takes to speak up and heal.

**RED FALCON PRESS**
CULTIVATE · ELEVATE · INNOVATE

**Publish with Red Falcon Press, imprint of Red Thread Publishing.**

We provide expert guidance to nonfiction authors through every stage of the publishing process. Visit **www.redthreadbooks.com** to learn more and connect with our team.

# REVIEW THIS BOOK

**Enjoyed** *The Empowerment Revolution*? Your feedback means the world! If the book resonated with you, inspired you, or offered something meaningful, we'd truly appreciate it if you left a review. Your feedback helps others discover the book—and it directly supports the author's work.

www.ingramcontent.com/pod-product-compliance
Lightning Source LLC
Chambersburg PA
CBHW021651120626
46545CB00002B/799